# THE
# SPONTANEOUS
# HEALING
## OF BELIEF

# ALSO BY GREGG BRADEN

## Books

*The Divine Matrix*
*The God Code*
*The Isaiah Effect\**
*Secrets of the Lost Mode of Prayer*
*Walking Between the Worlds\**
*Awakening to Zero Point\**

## CD Programs

*An Ancient Magical Prayer* (with Deepak Chopra)
*Awakening the Power of a Modern God*
*The Divine Matrix*
*The Divine Name* (with Jonathan Goldman)
*The Gregg Braden Audio Collection\**
*Speaking the Lost Language of God*
*The Spontaneous Healing of Belief*
*Unleashing the Power of the God Code*

*All the above are available from Hay House
except items marked with an asterisk

❀  ❀  ❀

Please visit Hay House USA: **www.hayhouse.com**®
Hay House Australia: **www.hayhouse.com.au**
Hay House UK: **www.hayhouse.co.uk**
Hay House South Africa: **www.hayhouse.co.za**
Hay House India: **www.hayhouse.co.in**

# THE
# SPONTANEOUS
# HEALING
## OF BELIEF

### SHATTERING THE PARADIGM
### OF FALSE LIMITS

## GREGG BRADEN

**HAY HOUSE, INC.**
Carlsbad, California • New York City
London • Sydney • Johannesburg
Vancouver • Hong Kong • New Delhi

*Published and distributed in the United States by:* Hay House, Inc.: www.hayhouse. com • *Published and distributed in Australia by:* Hay House Australia Pty. Ltd.: www. hayhouse.com.au • *Published and distributed in the United Kingdom by:* Hay House UK, Ltd.: www.hayhouse.co.uk • *Published and distributed in the Republic of South Africa by:* Hay House SA (Pty), Ltd.: www.hayhouse.co.za • *Distributed in Canada by:* Raincoast: www.raincoast.com • *Published in India by:* Hay House Publishers India: www.hayhouse.co.in

*Editorial consultation:* Stephanie Gunning • *Editorial supervision:* Jill Kramer
*Design:* Tricia Breidenthal

Grateful acknowledgment is made to reproduce an excerpt from *The Illuminated Rumi,* translations and commentary by Coleman Barks, Copyright © 1997. Reprinted courtesy of Broadway Books, an imprint of Random House, Inc.

Additional grateful acknowledgment is made for illustrations licensed through Dreamstime stock images, member of P.A.C.A. and C.E.P.I.C.

### Library of Congress Cataloging-in-Publication Data

Braden, Gregg.
  The spontaneous healing of belief : shattering the paradigm of false limits / Gregg Braden. -- 1st ed.
    p. cm.
  ISBN-13: 978-1-4019-1689-3 (hardcover)
  ISBN-13: 978-1-4019-1690-9 (tradepaper)   1.  Belief and doubt.  2.  Common fallacies.  3.  Contagion (Social psychology)  I. Title.
  BF773.B73 2008
  299'.93--dc22                                              2007039920


Hardcover ISBN: 978-1-4019-1689-3
Tradepaper ISBN: 978-1-4019-1690-9

11  10  09  08   5  4  3  2
1st edition, April 2008
2nd edition, April 2008

Printed in the United States of America

*In the instant of our first breath, we are infused
with the single greatest force in the universe—
the power to translate the possibilities of our minds
into the reality of our world. To fully awaken our
power, however, requires a subtle change in the
way we think of ourselves in life, a shift in <u>belief.</u>*

*Just the way sound creates visible waves as it travels
through a droplet of water, our "belief waves" ripple
through the quantum fabric of the universe to become
our bodies and the healing, abundance, and peace—
or disease, lack, and suffering—that we experience in
life. And just the way we can tune a sound to change
its patterns, we can tune our beliefs to preserve or
destroy all that we cherish, including life itself.*

*In a malleable world where everything from atoms
to cells is changing to match our beliefs, we're limited
only by the way we think of ourselves in that world.*

*This book is dedicated to our acceptance of such
an awesome power and our knowing that we are
never more than a belief away from our greatest
love, deepest healing, and most profound miracles.*

# CONTENTS

# INTRODUCTION

. . . . . . . . . . . . . . . . . . . . . . . . . . . . . . . . . . . . . . . . . .

*Let yourself be silently drawn by*
*the stronger pull of what you really love.*
— **Rumi** (c. 1207 c.e.–1273 c.e.), Sufi poet

. . . . . . . . . . . . . . . . . . . . . . . . . . . . . . . . . . . . . . . . . .

Pioneering physicist John Wheeler once said, "If you haven't found something strange during the day, it hasn't been much of a day."[1]

For a scientist, what could be any stranger than discovering that by simply watching our world in one place, we've somehow changed what happens somewhere else? . . . Yet this is precisely what the revelations of the new physics are showing us. As far back as 1935, Nobel Prize–winning physicist Albert Einstein acknowledged just how unsettling such quantum effects can be, calling them "spooky action at a distance." In a paper that he coauthored with noted physicists Boris Podolsky and Nathan Rosen, he stated, "No reasonable definition of reality could be expected to permit this [action at a distance]."[2]

Today, it's precisely these bizarre anomalies that have ignited a powerful revolution in the way we think of ourselves as well as the universe. For the better part of the 20th century, scientists struggled to understand what quantum strangeness is telling us about the way reality works. It's a documented fact, for example, that human consciousness influences quantum energy—*the stuff everything is made of*—under certain conditions. And that fact has opened the door to a possibility that pushes the limits of what we've been led to believe about our world in the past. A growing body of evidence now suggests that these unexpected results are more than just isolated exceptions. The question is: *How much* more?

Are the effects of observers in influencing their experiments actually a powerful window into the kind of reality we live in? And, if so, then we must ask, "Are those effects also telling us *who we are* within that reality?" The answer to both questions is yes: These are precisely the conclusions that the new discoveries suggest. They are also why I've written this book.

### There Are No Watchers

Scientists have shown that while *we may think* that we're only observing our world, in fact it's impossible for us to simply "watch" anything. Whether our attention is focused on a quantum particle during a laboratory experiment or anything else—from the healing of our bodies to the success of our careers and relationships—we have expectations and beliefs about what we're watching. Sometimes we're consciously aware of these preconceptions, but often we're not. It's these inner experiences that become part of what we're focused on. By "watching," we become part of what we're watching.

In the words of Wheeler, that makes us all "participators." The reason? When we focus our attention on a given place in a moment of time, we involve our consciousness. And in the vast field of consciousness, it appears that there's no clear boundary that tells us where *we* stop and the rest of the universe begins. When we think of the world in this way, it becomes clear why the ancients believed that everything is connected. As energy, it *is*.

As scientists continue to explore just what it means to be participators, new evidence points to an inescapable conclusion: that we live in an interactive reality where we change the world around us by changing what happens inside of us while we're watching—that is, our thoughts, feelings, and beliefs.

- **The Implication:** From the healing of disease, to the length of our lives, to the success of our careers and relationships, everything that we experience as "life" is directly linked to what we believe.

- **The Bottom Line:** To change our lives and relationships, heal our bodies, and bring peace to our families and nations requires a simple yet precise shift in the way we use belief.

For those who accept what science has led us to believe for the last 300 years, even to consider that our inner experience can affect reality is nothing short of heresy. The very idea blurs the safety zone that has traditionally separated science and spirituality—and us from our world. Rather than thinking of ourselves as passive victims in a place where, for example, things just "happen" for no apparent reason, such a consideration now places us squarely in the driver's seat of life.

In this position we find ourselves faced with undeniable evidence confirming that *we* are the architects of our reality. With this confirmation, we also see that we have the power to make disease obsolete and relegate war to a memory of our past. Suddenly, the key to catapulting our greatest dreams into reality is within our reach. It all comes back to *us:* Where do we fit into the universe? What is it that we're supposed to be doing in life?

> **Belief Code 1:**
> Experiments show that the focus of our attention changes reality itself and suggest that we live in an interactive universe.

What could be more important than answering these questions, understanding the implication of this revolution for our lives, and discovering what it means to *us?* In a world where the greatest crises of recorded human history now threaten our survival, the stakes couldn't be higher.

## The False Assumptions of Science

Although the revolution in the way we think of ourselves began nearly 100 years ago, it may not have been recognized by average people going about their daily routine. The change that it brings to our fast-paced lives of day planners, Internet relationships, and reality TV is happening on such a subtle level that few people may have even noticed that it's begun.

You probably haven't read about it in the morning newspaper, for example. It's unlikely that the question of "reality" has been the topic of conversation in your weekly staff meetings or at the office watercooler . . . that is, unless you're a scientist working to understand the nature of that reality. For *these* people, the revolution is akin to a huge earthquake that registers "off the scale"—while leveling some of the most sacred beliefs of science. Its effects are thundering through their laboratories, classrooms, and textbooks like a never-ending sonic boom. In its wake, it's leaving a wide swath of outdated teachings, along with the painful reevaluation of long-held beliefs and even entire careers.

Although it may seem to be quiet, the transformation that this reality revolution brings to our lives has erupted with a force unmatched by anything in the past, because the same discoveries that have sparked the questions have also led to the conclusion that the "facts" we've trusted for 300 years to explain the universe and our role in it are flawed. They're based on two assumptions that have been proven false:

- **False Assumption 1:** The space between "things" is empty. New discoveries now tell us that this is simply not true.

- **False Assumption 2:** Our inner experiences of feeling and belief have no effect on the world beyond our bodies. This has been proven absolutely wrong as well.

Paradigm-shattering experiments published in leading-edge, peer-reviewed journals reveal that we're bathed in a field of intelligent energy that fills what used to be thought of as empty space. Additional discoveries show beyond any reasonable doubt that this field responds to us—*it rearranges itself*—in the presence of our heart-based feelings and beliefs. And this is the revolution that changes everything.

It means that since the time when Isaac Newton's "laws" of physics were formalized in his 1687 release of *Philosophiae Naturalis Principia Mathematica* (Mathematical Principles of Natural Philosophy), we've based what we accept as our capabilities and limits on information that is false or, at the very least, incomplete. Since that time, most science has been grounded in the belief that we are insignificant in the overall scheme of things. It has written us right out of the equation of life and reality!

Is it any wonder that we often feel powerless to help our loved ones and ourselves when we face life's great crises? Is it at all surprising that we frequently feel just as helpless when we see our world changing so fast that it has been described as "falling apart at the seams"? Suddenly everything from personal capabilities and limitations to our collective reality is up for grabs. It's almost as if the conditions of our world are pushing us into the new frontier of consciousness itself, forcing us to rediscover who we are in order to survive what we've created.

The reason why you are a powerful key in this revolution is that it's based entirely on something that you and I are doing right now, in this very moment. Alone and together, individually and collectively, consciously and unconsciously, we are all choosing the way we think of ourselves and *what we believe* to be true of our world. The results of our beliefs surround us as our everyday experience.

The revolution of scientific understanding suggests that from our personal health and relationships to global war and peace, the reality of our lives is nothing more and nothing less than our "belief waves" shaping the quantum stuff that everything is made from. It's all related to what we accept about our world, our capabilities, our limits, and ourselves.

### The Undeniable Facts

"Okay," you're saying, "we've heard all of this before. It's naïve, and maybe even arrogant, to suggest that the universe is in any way affected by our personal beliefs. It just can't be that simple." Twenty years ago, as a scientist trained in the conventional ways science has viewed our world in the past, I would have agreed with you.

At first blush there appears to be nothing in our traditional way of seeing the world that allows for our inner beliefs to do much of anything at all, let alone change the universe itself—that is, however, until we begin to examine what the new discoveries are showing us. Although the results of reality-bending research have been published in leading technical journals, they are often shared in the vocabulary of "scientification" that masks the power of their meaning to a non-scientific person.

And that's where our revolution comes in. Suddenly, we don't *need* the language of science to tell us that we're a powerful part of our world. Our everyday lives *show* us that we are. What I believe we *are* asking for, however, are the keys to applying our power to what happens in our world.

I suspect that future generations will see our time in history as the turning point when the conditions of the planet forced us to discover how the universe really works and accept our interactive role in it. Rather than following the first three centuries of scientific imagery that has portrayed us as powerless victims in life, the new science suggests we are just the opposite. In the late 1990s and early 2000s, research has revealed the following facts:

- **Fact 1:** The universe, our world, and our bodies are made of a shared field of energy that was scientifically recognized in the 20th century and is now identified by names that include the field, the quantum hologram, the mind of God, nature's mind, and the Divine Matrix.[3]

- **Fact 2:** In the field of the Divine Matrix, "things" that have been connected physically and then separated act as if they are still linked, through a phenomenon known as *entanglement*.[4]

- **Fact 3:** Human DNA directly influences what happens in the Divine Matrix in a way that appears to defy the laws of time and space.[5]

- **Fact 4:** Human belief (and the feelings and emotions surrounding it) directly changes the DNA that affects what occurs in the Divine Matrix.[6]

- **Fact 5:** When we shift our beliefs about our bodies and our world, the Divine Matrix translates that change into the reality of our lives.[7, 8]

With these and similar discoveries in mind, we must ask ourselves the question that is perhaps the most revealing of all: *Are we born with the natural ability to create and modify our bodies and the world?* If so, then we must be willing to pose an even more difficult question: *What responsibility do we have to use our power in the presence of what are arguably the greatest threats to the future of our lives, our world, and even our species?*

### Now Is the Time

Clearly we don't know all there is to know about how the universe works and our role in it. While new studies will undoubtedly reveal greater insights, we could wait for another hundred years and still not have all of the answers. A growing consensus of scientists suggest that we may not have that long.

Powerful voices in the scientific community, such as Sir Martin Rees, professor of astrophysics at the University of Cambridge, suggest that we have only a "50/50" chance of surviving the 21st century without a major setback.[9] While we've always had natural disasters to contend with, a new class of threats that Rees calls "human induced" now have to be taken into account as well.

Emerging studies, such as those reported in *Scientific American*'s special issue entitled "Crossroads for Planet Earth" (September 2005), echo Rees's warning, telling us: "The next 50 years will be decisive in determining whether the human race—*now entering a unique period in its history*—can ensure the best possible future for itself [my emphasis]."[10]

In a series of essays written by experts in fields that range from global health and energy consumption to sustainable lifestyles, the general agreement is that we simply can't continue with the way we use energy, the direction of technology, and an ever-expanding population if we expect to survive another hundred years. Complicating all of these problems is the growing threat of a world war that is driven, at least in part, by the competition for the same disappearing resources that defined the essays. Perhaps the uniqueness of our time is best described by Harvard University biologist E. O. Wilson. He states that we are about to enter what he calls the "bottleneck" in time, when both our resources and our ability to solve the problems of our day will be pushed to their limits.

The good news echoed by the experts, however, is that "if decision makers can get the framework right, the future of humanity will be secured by thousands of mundane decisions. . . . It is usually in mundane matters that the most profound advances are made."[11] Without a doubt, there are countless choices that each of us will be asked to make in the near future. I can't help but think, though, that one of the most profound—and perhaps the simplest—will be the decision to embrace what the new science has shown us about who we are and our place in the universe.

If we can accept the powerful evidence that consciousness itself and our role in it are the missing links in the theories of how reality works, then everything changes. In that change, we begin anew. This makes us part of, rather than separate from, all that we see and experience.

And that's why this revolution is so powerful. It writes us—all of humankind—right back into the equation of the universe. It also casts us into the role of solving the great crises of our day, rather than leaving them to a future generation or simply to fate. As we are architects of our reality, with the power to rearrange the atoms of matter itself, what problem cannot be solved and what solution could possibly be beyond our reach?

### The Power to Choose Is the Power to Change

The prospect of relying on something *within us* to meet the challenges of our time, as opposed to depending on the science and technology of our outer world, can be a little unsettling for some people. "How do we learn to do something so powerful and so necessary?" is the question that often arises. It's usually followed by another: "If this is the way of the future, how do we learn now—and do so fast?" Perhaps both of these questions are best answered in the words of the 20th-century philosopher and poet Kahlil Gibran.

In his classic book *The Prophet,* Gibran reminds us of what it means to have a great gift and to know that its power is already within us. He states: "No man can reveal to you aught but that which already lies half asleep in the dawning of your knowledge."[12] In words that are as beautiful today as they were when they were first published in 1923, Gibran tells us that we can't be taught what we don't already know. And we came into the world already knowing how to use our beliefs.

So this book is less about learning to rewrite the code of reality, and more about accepting that we already have power to do so— something that has been explored by many mystics in the past, including the ancient Sufi poet Jalal ad-Din ar-Rumi. "What strange beings we are," says Rumi, "that sitting in hell at the bottom of the dark, we're afraid of our own immortality."[13] With these words, the great mystic describes the irony of our mysterious condition in this world.

On the one hand, we're told that we are frail and powerless beings who live in a world where things just "happen" for no apparent reason. On the other hand, our most ancient and cherished spiritual traditions tell us that there's a force that lives within every one of us, a power that nothing in the world can touch. With it comes the promise of surviving the darkest moments of life and the reassurance that difficult times are only a part of a journey that leads to a place where bad things can't happen any longer. It's no wonder that we feel confused, helpless, and sometimes even angry as we witness the suffering of our loved ones and share the agony of what sometimes seems like hell in the world around us.

So which is it? Are we hopelessly fragile victims of events that are beyond our control, or are we powerful creators harboring dormant abilities that we are only beginning to understand? The answer may reveal the truth of one of the deepest mysteries of our past. It is also the focus of some of the greatest controversy in scientific discussions today. The reason? Both questions have the same answer: *Yes!*

Yes, we are occasionally victims of circumstance. And yes, we are sometimes the powerful creators of those same circumstances. Which of these roles we experience is determined by choices that we make in our lives, *choices based upon our beliefs.* Through the godlike power of human belief, we are given the equally divine ability to bring *what* we believe to life in the matrix of energy that bathes and surrounds us.

### Why This Book?

As I was writing *The Divine Matrix* (Hay House, 2007), it was immediately clear that our role in the acceptance of miracles could easily become lost as a sidebar in the overall message of the book. To describe the language of belief and how it allows us to be the architects of our lives would require another volume.

Within these pages, you'll discover how to heal the false beliefs that may have limited you in the past. In addition, you will . . .

- . . . identify the beliefs that reverse disease in your body.

- . . . learn the ones that create lasting, nurturing relationships in your life.

- . . . uncover those that bring peace to your life, your family, your community, and your world.

As different as peace, relationships, and healing may appear to be from one another, they're all based in the same principle: the "language" of belief and the feelings that we have about what we believe.

By its nature, the exploration of belief is a journey that is deeply personal. Each of us has a little different take on our own beliefs, while finding a way for them to fit into the greater collective ones of our culture, religious teachings, family, and friends. Since it's such an experience, there are probably as many ideas on what belief is as there are people having them.

Throughout the seven concise chapters in this book, I'm inviting you into a new and possibly very different way of thinking about yourself, your life, and your world. For some, this way of seeing things is a challenge to everything they've been taught. For others, it piques their curiosity just enough to begin a new path of self-discovery.

For everyone, it's important to know up front what you can expect from the information that follows. If you're like me, you like to know where you're going before you begin the journey. For that reason, I've described precisely what this book is—and what it is *not:*

— **This *is not* a science book.** Although I will share the leading-edge science that invites us to rethink our relationship to the world, this work has not been written to conform to the format or standards of a classroom science text or a technical journal.

— **This *is not* a peer-reviewed research paper.** Each chapter and every report of research *has not* gone through the lengthy review process of a certified board or selected panel of "experts" with a history of seeing our world through the eyes of a single field of study, such as physics, math, or psychology.

— **This *is* a well-researched and well-documented guide.** It has been written in a reader-friendly way that describes the experiments, case studies, historical records, and personal experiences that support an empowering way of seeing ourselves in the world.

— **This *is* an example of what can be accomplished when we cross the traditional boundaries of science and spirituality.** Rather than viewing the problems of our time through the eyes of nature, artificially separated and isolated as physics, chemistry, or history, it is designed to bridge the gap between the best science of today and the timeless wisdom of our past, weaving the two together into a greater understanding of our role in life. The aim in doing so is that we may apply this knowledge to create a better world—and discover more about ourselves along the way.

*The Spontaneous Healing of Belief* is written with one purpose in mind: to share an empowering message of hope and possibility in a world where we are often led to feel hopeless and powerless.

### Do We Really Want the Truth?

In another of his writings, Rumi further described the curious nature of our relationship to reality, saying, "We are the mirror, and the face in the mirror. We are the sweet cold water, *and* the jar that pours [the water]." Similar to the way Jesus told us that we might save ourselves by bringing forth that which is within us, Rumi reminds us that we are continually creating reality (sometimes consciously and sometimes *un*consciously) and are doing so *while* we experience what we have created. In other words, we are the artists as well as the art, suggesting that we have the power to modify and change our lives today, while also choosing how we fashion them anew tomorrow.

While for some people these empowering analogies are a refreshing new way to view the world, for others they shake the foundation of long-held, traditional assumptions. It's not unusual to see prominent scientists who are reluctant to acknowledge the implications of their own research when it reveals that we are, in fact, powerful creators in the universe.

When I share this irony with live audiences, it's often received with a response that echoes a classic line from the film *A Few Good Men*. In the powerful 1992 drama, when Guantánamo Bay base commander Colonel Nathan Jessep (played by Jack Nicholson) is subject to courtroom examination by Lieutenant Daniel Kaffee (played by Tom Cruise), he is asked for the *truth* regarding the mysterious death of a U.S. serviceman at the base. Acknowledging that his answer would be too much for the people in the courtroom to bear, Jessep responds with the timeless words: "You can't *handle* the truth!"

Perhaps the greatest challenge of our time in history is simply this: *Can we handle the truth that we have asked ourselves to discover?* Do we have the courage to accept who we are in the universe and the role that our existence implies? If the answer is yes, then we must also accept the responsibility that comes with knowing that we can change the world by changing ourselves.

We've already seen that the widely held beliefs of hate, separation, and fear can destroy our bodies and our world faster than we could have ever imagined. Maybe all we need is a little shift in the way we think of ourselves in order to recognize the great truth that we are, in fact, the architects of our experience. We are cosmic artists expressing our deepest beliefs on the quantum canvas of the universe. What are the chances that by transforming the destructive beliefs of our past into life-affirming ones of healing and peace, we can change the world of today and the future as well?

We may not have to ask ourselves this question much longer. New discoveries about the power of belief suggest that we're about to find out.

— **Gregg Braden**
Taos, New Mexico

### CHAPTER ONE

# A New View of Reality:
# The Universe as a
# Consciousness Computer

*"The history of the universe is, in effect, a huge and ongoing quantum computation. The universe is a quantum computer."*
— **Seth Lloyd,** MIT professor and designer
of the first feasible quantum computer

*"A long time ago, the Great Programmer wrote a program that runs all possible universes on His Big Computer."*
— **Jürgen Schmidhuber,** pioneer in artificial intelligence

We live our lives based on what we believe. When we think about the truth of this statement, we immediately recognize a startling reality: Beyond anything else that we may actually *do* in our lives, the beliefs that precede our actions are the foundation of all that we cherish, dream, become, and accomplish.

From the morning rituals that we go through to greet the world each day, to the inventions that we use to make our lives better, to the technology that destroys life through war—our personal routines, community customs, religious ceremonies, and entire civilizations

**Belief Code 2:**
We live our lives based on what we believe about our world, ourselves, our capabilities, and our limits.

are based on our beliefs. Not only do our beliefs provide the structure for the way we live our lives, now the same areas of study that have discounted our inner experiences in the past are showing us that the way we *feel* about the world around us is a force that extends *into* that world.

In this way, science is catching up with our most cherished spiritual and indigenous traditions, which have always told us that our world is nothing more than a reflection of what we accept in our beliefs.

With access to such a power already within us, to say that our beliefs are important to life is an understatement. Our beliefs *are* life! They are where it begins and how it sustains itself. From our immune response and the hormones that regulate and balance our bodies . . . to our ability to heal bones, organs, and skin—and even conceive life—the role of human belief is rapidly taking center stage in the new frontiers of quantum biology and physics.

If our beliefs hold so much power, and if we live our lives based on what we believe, then the obvious question is: *Where do our beliefs come from?* The answer may surprise you.

With few exceptions, they originate with what science, history, religion, culture, and family tell us. In other words, the essence of our capabilities and limits may well be based in what *other people* tell us. That realization leads to the next question that we must ask ourselves:

*If our lives are based on what we believe,*
*then what if those beliefs are wrong?*

What if we're living our lives shrouded in the false limitations and incorrect assumptions that other people have formed over generations, centuries, or even millennia?

Historically, for example, we've been taught that we are insignificant specks of life passing through a brief moment in time, limited by the "laws" of space, atoms, and DNA. This view suggests that we'll have little effect on anything during our stay in this world, and when we're gone, the universe will never even notice our absence.

While the words of this description may sound a bit harsh, the general idea isn't so far from what many of us today have been conditioned to hold true. It's precisely these beliefs that often leave us feeling small and helpless in the face of life's greatest challenges.

What if we're more than this? Could it be that we're really very powerful beings in disguise? What if we're delegates of miraculous potential, born into this world with capabilities beyond our wildest dreams—ones that we've simply forgotten under the conditions that have shocked us into the dreamlike state of being powerless?

How would our lives change, for instance, if we discovered that we're born with the power to reverse disease? Or what if we could *choose* the peace in our world, the abundance in our lives, and how long we live? What if we found that the universe itself is directly affected by a power that we've hidden from ourselves for so long that we've forgotten it's even ours?

Such a radical discovery would change everything. It would alter what we believe about ourselves, the universe, and our role within it. It's also precisely what the leading-edge discoveries of our day are showing us.

For centuries, there have been people who refused to accept the limitations that have traditionally defined what it means to live in this world. They refused to believe that we just appear through a mysterious birth that defies explanation. They rejected the idea that such a miraculous emergence could be for the purpose of living in suffering, pain, and loneliness until we leave this world just as mysteriously as we arrived.

To answer their yearning for a greater truth, they had to venture beyond the boundaries of their conditioning. They isolated themselves—from friends, family, and community—and let go, *really let go,* of what they had been taught about the world. And when they did, something precious and beautiful happened in their lives: They discovered a new freedom for themselves that opened the door of possibilities for others. It all began by their asking the question that was just as bold in their time as it is in ours: *What if our beliefs are wrong?*

As we'll see in the story of the yogi that follows, it's in our absolute surrender to such a possibility that we discover the freedom that tells us who we really are. My personal belief, however, is that we don't have to live in a cold, damp cave in the middle of nowhere to find it. I also feel that personal liberation begins with the individual commitment to know who we are in the universe. When we make such a commitment, everything from the way we think of ourselves to the way we love will change. They must, because *we* are changed in the presence of these deeper understandings.

It all comes back to what we believe.

While it may sound too simple to be true, I'm convinced that the universe works precisely in this way.

### A Miracle Set in Stone

In the 11th century c.e., the great Tibetan yogi Milarepa began a personal retreat to master his body, a journey that would last until his death at the age of 84. Earlier in his life, Milarepa had already acquired many seemingly miraculous yogic abilities, such as the power to use "psychic heat" to warm his body in the harsh Tibetan winters.

After suffering the unbearable pain of losing his family and friends at the hands of village rivals, he employed his mystic arts for purposes of retribution and revenge. In doing so, he killed many people and struggled to find meaning in what he had done. One day he realized that he had misused the gift of his yogic and psychic abilities, so he went into seclusion to find healing through even greater mastery. In sharp contrast to the life of material abundance he had known before, Milarepa soon discovered that he needed no contact with the outside world. He became a recluse.

After exhausting his initial supplies of food, Milarepa found himself surviving on the nourishment of the meager vegetation near his cave. For many years, the nettle plants that grow in the arid expanses of Tibet's high desert were all he ate. Without any substantial food, clothing, or companionship to interrupt his inner focus, Milarepa lived for years on almost nothing. His only human contact was the occasional pilgrim who stumbled upon the cave that sheltered him. The reports of those who did happen to find him by accident described a frightening sight.

The little clothing with which he'd originally started his retreat had weathered into sparse shreds of cloth that left him virtually naked. Due to the lack of nutrition in his diet, Milarepa had shrunk to little more than a living skeleton, with his long hair, as well as his skin, turning a dull green from the overdose of chlorophyll. He looked like a walking ghost! The deprivation that he imposed upon himself, although extreme, did lead him to his goal of yogic mastery. Before his death in 1135 c.e., Milarepa left proof of his freedom from the physical world in the form of a miracle that modern scientists say should simply not be possible.

During a group pilgrimage to Tibet in the spring of 1998, I chose a route that would lead us directly to Milarepa's cave and the miracle that he left behind. I wanted to see the place where he breached the laws of physics to free us from our limited beliefs.

Nineteen days after this trip began, I found myself in the great yogi's retreat, standing precisely where he had stood nearly 900 years before. With my face only inches away from the wall of the cave, I was staring squarely into the mystery that Milarepa left behind.

Milarepa's cave is one of those places that you have to know how to find in order to get there. It's not somewhere you would just happen upon during a casual jaunt through Tibet. I first heard about the famous yogi from a Sikh mystic who became my yoga teacher in the 1980s. For years I'd studied the mystery surrounding Milarepa's renunciation of all worldly possessions, his journey throughout the sacred plateau of central Tibet, and what he discovered as a devoted mystic. All of the study led to this moment in his cave.

I stared in wonder at the smooth, black walls that surrounded me and could only imagine what it would be like inhabiting such a cold, dark, and remote place for so many years. While Milarepa had lived in as many as 20 different retreats throughout his time in solitude, it was his meeting with a student in this particular cave that set it apart from the others.

To demonstrate his yogic mastery, Milarepa performed two feats that skeptics have never duplicated. The first was moving his hand through the air with such speed and force that he created the "shock wave" of a sonic boom reverberating against the rock throughout the cavern. (I attempted this on my own, with no luck.) The second feat was the one that I had waited nearly 15 years, traveled halfway around the world, and acclimated to some of the world's highest elevations for 19 days to see.

To demonstrate his mastery over the limits of the physical world, Milarepa had placed his open hand against the cave's wall at about shoulder level . . . *and then continued to push his hand farther into the rock in front of him,* as if the wall did not exist! When he did so, the stone beneath his palm became soft and malleable, leaving the deep impression of his hand for all to see. When the student who witnessed this marvel tried to do the same thing, it's recorded that all he had to show for it was the frustration of an injured hand.

As I opened my palm and placed it into the impression of Milarepa's, I could feel my fingertips cradled in the form of the yogi's hand in the precise position that his fingers had assumed hundreds of years earlier—a feeling that was both humbling and inspiring at the same time. The fit was so perfect that any doubt I had about the authenticity of the handprint quickly disappeared. Immediately, my thoughts turned to the man himself. I wanted to know what was happening to him when he merged with that rock. What was he thinking? *What was he feeling?* How did he defy the physical "laws" telling us that two "things" (his hand and the rock) can't occupy the same place at the same time?

In anticipation of my questions, our Tibetan translator, Xjin-la (not his real name), answered before I even asked them. "He has belief," he stated in a matter-of-fact voice. "The *geshe* [great teacher] believes that he and the rock are not separate." I was fascinated by the way our 20th-century guide spoke of the 900-year-old yogi in the present tense, as if he were in the room with us. "His meditation teaches him that he is part of the rock. The rock cannot contain him. To the geshe, this cave is not a wall, so he can move freely as if the rock does not exist."

"Did he leave this impression to demonstrate his mastery for himself?" I asked.

"No," Xjin-la replied. "The geshe does not need to prove anything to himself. The yogi lived in this place for many years, but we see only one handprint." I looked around for signs of others somewhere in the shallow cave. Our guide was right—I didn't see any. "The hand in the rock is *not* for the geshe," our guide continued. "It is for his student."

It made perfect sense. When Milarepa's disciple saw his master do something that tradition and other teachers said could not happen, it helped him break through his beliefs about what is possible. He saw his teacher's mastery with his own eyes. And because he witnessed the miracle personally, his experience told his mind that he wasn't limited or bound by the "laws" of reality as they were known at the time.

By being in the presence of such a miracle, Milarepa's student was confronted with the same dilemma that everyone faces in choosing to free themselves from the limits of their own beliefs: He had to reconcile the personal experience of his teacher's miracle with what those around him believed—the "laws" that they accepted describing how the universe operates.

The dilemma is this: The worldview that was embraced by the family, friends, and people of the student's day asked him to accept one way of seeing the universe and how things work. This included the belief that the rock of a cave wall is a barrier to the flesh of a human body. On the other hand, the student had just been shown that there are exceptions to such "laws." The irony was that both ways of seeing the world were absolutely correct. Each depended on how someone chose to think of it in a given moment of time.

I asked myself: *Could the same thing be happening in our lives today?* As far-fetched as this question may sound in light of our scientific knowledge and technological advances, modern scientists are beginning to describe a similar irony. Using the language of quantum physics rather than evidence of yogic miracles, a growing number of leading-edge scientists suggest that the universe and everything in it "is" what it "is" *because* of the force of consciousness itself: our beliefs and what we accept as the reality of our world. Interestingly, the more we understand the relationship between our inner experiences and our world, the less far-fetched this suggestion becomes.

While the story of Milarepa's cave is a powerful example of one man's journey to discover his relationship to the world, we don't need to seclude ourselves in a cave and eat nettles until we turn green to discover the same truth for ourselves! The scientific discoveries of the last 150 years have already shown that the relationship between consciousness, reality, and belief exists.

Are we willing to accept the relationship we've been shown and the responsibility that comes with such power so that we can apply it in our lives in a meaningful way? Only through the future that is on the horizon will we know how we've answered this question.

### We Know There Are Things We Don't Know

During a press conference at NATO headquarters in Belgium in June 2002, then U.S. Secretary of Defense Donald Rumsfeld described the status of intelligence and information gathering in a post-9/11 world, famously stating, ". . . there are known knowns; there are things we know we know. We also know there are known unknowns; that is to say we know there are some things we do not know. But there are also unknown unknowns—the ones we don't know we don't know."[1]

In other words, Rumsfeld was saying that we don't have all of the information and we *know* that we don't have it. While this now-famous speech was directed toward American intelligence gathering for the war on terror, the same can be said of the state of scientific knowledge today.

As successful as science has been in revealing the answers to our deepest mysteries, some of the greatest minds of our time openly suggest that the language of science is incomplete. In 2002, a journal in the Nature Publishing Group featured an editorial describing the virtues of the scientific method that stated: "By its nature, even at its most exact and profound, science is incomplete in its explanations, but self-correcting as it steers itself away from the occasional wrong path."[2] Although the "self-correcting" of scientific ideas may occur eventually, sometimes it takes hundreds of years to do so, as the argument of whether or not the universe is connected by a field of energy demonstrates.

> **Belief Code 3:**
> Science is a language—
> one of many that describe
> us, the universe, our bodies,
> and how things work.

This limitation is not unique to a single branch of study such as physics or mathematics. Twentieth-century physician and poet Lewis Thomas, for example, stated that in real life, "every field of science is incomplete." He attributed the gaps in our knowledge to the youth of science itself, asserting, "Whatever the record of accomplishment during the last 200 years [most fields of science] are still in their very earliest stages."[3]

Admittedly, there are huge gaps in our scientific ability to describe why things are the way they are. Using the language of science, for example, physicists believe they have successfully identified the four fundamental forces of nature and the universe: *gravity, electromagnetism,* and the *strong* and *weak nuclear forces.* While we know enough about these forces to apply them to technology ranging from microcircuits to space travel, we also know that our understanding of them is still incomplete. We can say that with certainty, because scientists have still not been able to find the elusive key that combines these four forces into a single description of how our universe works: *a unified field theory.*

Although new theories, such as the superstring theory, may ultimately hold the answer, critics have posed a good question that has yet to be answered. The string theories of the 1970s, which eventually became the superstring theory that was formally accepted in 1984, were all developed more than 20 years ago. If the theories really work, then why are they still "theories"? With hundreds of the planet's best minds and the greatest computing power in the history of the world, why has the superstring theory failed to successfully marry the four forces of nature into a single story that tells us how the universe works?

Without question, this was one of the great disappointments that haunted Einstein until the end of his life. In a 1951 letter to his friend Maurice Solovine, the great theoretical physicist confided his frustration. "The unified field theory has been put into retirement," he begins. "It is so difficult to employ mathematically that I have not been able to verify it somehow, in spite of all my efforts."[4]

It may not be surprising that the science of today doesn't have all the answers. The quantum discoveries of the last century have led to a surprising and radical new way for us to think of ourselves and how the universe works. This novel way of thinking is so radical, in fact, that it flies directly in the face of what science has asked us to believe for nearly 300 years. So rather than building upon the certainty of what was believed in the past, the new discoveries have forced scientists to rethink their assumptions of how the universe works. In some ways, they've had to go back to square one. Probably the biggest shift in thinking has been the realization that matter itself—the stuff that everything is made of—doesn't even exist in the way we used to think it did.

Rather than thinking of the universe as being made of "things"—such as atoms, for example—that are separate and have little effect on other things, quantum theories suggest that the universe and our bodies are made of ever-changing fields of energy, which interact with one another to create our world in ways that can only be described as possibilities rather than certainties. This is important to us because we are part of the energy that is doing the interacting. And it's our awareness of this fact that changes *everything.*

When we recognize that we're enmeshed in the dance of energy that bathes creation, that realization changes who we believe we are, what we've always thought the universe is, and how we believe our world works. Perhaps most important, it transforms our role from that of passive observers to powerful agents of change interacting with the same stuff everything else is made of. And our view of where that stuff comes from is itself changing very quickly.

### Particles, Possibilities, and Consciousness: A Brief Look at Quantum Reality

In Newton's mechanical view of the cosmos, the universe is thought of in terms of particles whose behavior can be known and predicted at any moment in time. It's like balls on a pool table: If we have the information that describes the force of a ball as it strikes another (speed, angle, and so on), then we should be able to predict where and how the one that has been struck will travel. And if it should hit other balls in its journey, we'll know where and how fast they're traveling as well. The key here is that the mechanical view of the universe sees the smallest units of the stuff our world is made of as *things*.

Quantum physics looks at the universe differently. In recent years, scientists have developed the technology that has made it possible to document the strange and sometimes miraculous behavior of the quantum energy that forms the essence of the universe and our bodies. For example:

- Quantum energy can exist in two very different forms: as visible particles or invisible waves. The energy is still there either way, just making itself known in different forms.

- A quantum particle can be in one place only, two places at once, or even many places simultaneously. The interesting thing, however, is that no matter how far apart these locations appear to be physically, the particle acts as if it's still connected.

- Quantum particles can communicate with themselves at different points in time. They're not limited by the concepts of past, present, and future. To a quantum particle, then is now and there is here.

These things are important because we're made of the same quantum particles that can behave miraculously when given the right conditions. The question is this: *If quantum particles are not limited by the "laws" of science—at least as we know them today—and we're made of the same particles, then can* <u>*we*</u> *do miraculous things as well?* In other words, is the behavior that physicists call "anomalous" demonstrating our scientific limits, or is it really showing us something else? Could the freedom in time and space that these particles show us be revealing to us the freedom that is possible in our lives?

Following all of the research, documentation, and direct experience of those who have transcended the limits of their own beliefs, without reservation I believe that the answer is a solid *yes*.

The only difference between those isolated particles and us is that we're made of lots of them, linked through the mysterious stuff that fills the places we used to think of as "empty space"—a form of energy that we're only beginning to understand. It's the recent acknowledgment of this strange form of energy in mainstream science that has catapulted us into a new and almost holistic way of seeing ourselves in the universe.

❀

**Belief Code 4:**
If the particles that we're made of can be in instantaneous communication with one another, be in two places at once, and even change the past through choices made in the present, then we can as well.

In 1944, Max Planck, the man many consider to be the father of quantum theory, shocked the world by saying that there is a "matrix" of energy that provides the blueprint for our physical world.[5] In this place of pure energy, everything begins, from the birth of stars and DNA to our deepest relationships, peace between nations, and personal healing. The willingness to embrace the matrix's existence in mainstream science is still so new that scientists have yet to agree upon a single name for it.

Some simply call it the "field." Others have referred to it with terms that range from the technical-sounding "quantum hologram" to almost spiritual-seeming names, such as the "mind of God" and "nature's mind." In my 2007 book describing the history and proof of the field, I echoed the bridging effect that it has had between science and spirituality, referring to it as the *Divine Matrix.* The experimental proof that Planck's matrix is real now provides the missing link that bridges our spiritual experiences of belief, imagination, and prayer with the miracles that we see in the world around us.

The reason why Planck's words are so powerful is because they forever changed the way we think of our bodies, our world, and our role in the universe. They imply that we're much more than simply the "observers" that scientists have described, passing through a brief moment of time in a creation that already exists. Through the connection that joins all things, the experiments have now shown that we directly affect the waves and particles of the universe. In short, the universe responds to our beliefs. It is this difference—thinking of us as powerful creators rather than passive observers—that has become the crux of some of the greatest controversy among some of the greatest minds in recent history. The implications are absolutely staggering.

In a quote from his autobiographical notes, for example, Albert Einstein shared his belief that we have little effect on the universe as a whole and are lucky if we can understand even a small part of it. We live in a world, he said, "which exists independently of us human beings and which stands before us like a great, eternal riddle, at least partially accessible to our inspection and thinking."[6]

In contrast to Einstein's perspective, which is still widely held by many scientists today, John Wheeler, an honored Princeton physicist and colleague of Einstein, offers a radically different view of our role in creation. Wheeler's studies have led him to believe that we may live in a universe where consciousness is not only important, but also actually creative—in other words, a "participatory universe."

Clarifying his belief, Wheeler says, "We could not even imagine a universe that did not somewhere and for some stretch of time contain observers because the very building materials of the universe are these acts of observer-participancy."[7]

What a shift! In a completely revolutionary interpretation of our relationship to the world, Wheeler is stating that it's impossible for us simply to watch the world happen around us. We can never be observers, because when we observe, we create and modify what is created. Sometimes the effect of our observation is nearly undetectable; and, as we'll discover in later chapters, sometimes it's not. Either way, the discoveries of the last century suggest that our act of observing the world is an act of creation unto itself. And it's consciousness that's doing the creating!

These findings seem to support Wheeler's proposition that we can no longer think of ourselves merely as onlookers who have no effect on the world that we're observing. When we view "life"—our spiritual and material abundance, our relationships and careers, our deepest loves and greatest achievements, as well as our fears and the lack of all of these things—we may also be looking squarely at the mirror of our truest and sometimes most unconscious beliefs.

### Architects of Life

Through our beliefs, we're the bridge between reality and all that we could ever imagine. It's the power of what we truly believe about ourselves that gives life to our highest aspirations and greatest dreams, the things that make the universe as it is. And if the whole universe sounds like a place too big to even think about, that's okay—we can start by simply thinking about ourselves and our everyday world.

Consider your relationship to the room you're sitting in. While you're thinking, ask yourself these questions: *What role did I play to get myself here? How did I arrive at this precise place in this precise moment?* Then consider how time, space, energy, and matter have all converged in a mysterious and precious way to bring you to this very moment, and ask: *Is it just an accident?*

Are you merely a fluke of biology, energy, and matter that just happened to converge in this instant? If your answer to this question is *No!* then you're really going to like what comes next. Because if you honestly believe that you're more than an accident of time, space, and energy, then do you really think that you would find yourself in a world of so many quantum possibilities without a way to choose from among those possibilities?

To acknowledge that we play a central role in how our everyday reality turns out is to acknowledge that we're somehow interacting with the essence of the universe. For such a thing to be possible, it means that we must also recognize the following:

When we choose to embark upon a different career path or a new relationship or to heal a life-threatening disease, we're really rewriting the code of reality. If we think about all the implications of all the decisions we make in each moment of every day, it becomes clear how our seemingly little choices can have effects that reach far beyond our personal lives. In a universe where each experience is built upon the outcome of previous ones, it's obvious that *all* are necessary. There are no "wasted" choices, because every event and decision is required. Each must be precisely where it is before the others can follow.

> **Belief Code 5:**
> Our beliefs have the power to change the flow of events in the universe— literally to interrupt and redirect time, matter, and space, and the events that occur within them.

Suddenly, our choice to help someone who's lost in the airport, for example, or our willingness to understand our anger before we unleash it on those who don't deserve it takes on new meaning. Each choice sets into motion a ripple current that will affect not only our lives, but also the world beyond.

So, think of all the things that had to happen from a time before you were even born for you to be in the precise place that you are in this moment. Think of the unfathomable number of tiny particles of star dust that originated with the birth of the universe. Contemplate where those particles have been, and consider how they've come together in just the right way to become the "you" that you are today. In doing so, you find it becomes abundantly clear that something— *some intelligent force*—is holding the particles of *you* together right now, as you read the words on this page.

That force is what makes our beliefs so powerful. If we can communicate with it, then we can change how the particles of "us" behave in the world. We can rewrite the code of our reality.

A growing number of mainstream scientists are now drawing parallels between the way the universe works and the output of a huge and incredibly ancient computer simulation—a literal virtual reality. In this comparison, our everyday world is thought of as a simulation that operates in much the way the "holodeck" did in *Star Trek: The Next Generation*, a TV series that first aired in 1987. It's an experience that's created within the container of a greater reality for the purpose of mastering the conditions of that reality.

Taking this just one step further, we can imagine that if we understand the rules of this ancient and ongoing reality program, then we can understand how to change the conditions of fear, war, and disease that have hurt us in the past. In such a way of thinking, everything takes on a whole new meaning. As speculative and science fiction–ish as such a proposition may sound, it's only one of the implications that stem directly from this powerful new way of thinking of the universe.

But first things first: Let's go back to the whole idea of reality as a program. Just how can something as big as the entire universe be the output of a computer?

The simplicity of what follows may surprise you. . . .

### The Universe as a Consciousness Computer

In the 1940s Konrad Zuse (pronounced *zoo-sŭh*), the man credited with developing the first computers, had a flash of insight into the way the universe may work. When he did so, he also gave us a new way of thinking about our role in creation. While he was developing the programs to run his early computers, he asked a question that sounds more like something out of the plot of a novel than an idea meant to be taken as a serious scientific possibility.

Zuse's question was simply this: *Is it possible that the entire universe operates as a big computer, with a code that makes whatever is possible, possible?* Or, perhaps even more bizarre, he wondered if a form of cosmic computing machinery is continually creating the universe and everything in it. *In other words, are we living a virtual reality running on a really big computer made of quantum energy itself?* This is clearly a huge question with implications that rattle everything from the ideas of life and evolution to the basis of religion itself. Also, it spawned the hugely popular 1999 film *The Matrix*.

Zuse was obviously a man ahead of his time. Thirty years later, he elaborated on these ideas in his book *Calculating Space* and set into motion the events that led to the revolution in our view of reality and everyday life.[8] Commenting on how his mind-blowing insights took shape, Zuse described how he made the connection between the machines that he was building and the machinery of the universe. "It happened that in contemplating causality [the relationship between things that happen and what causes those things to happen]," he said, "I suddenly thought to interpret the cosmos as a gigantic calculating machine."[9]

The bottom line of this way of seeing the universe is that whether we're talking about rocks and trees, the ocean, or you and me, *everything* is information. And just as any information can be the output of processes that put it all together, the universe is really the product of a very big program that began long ago. While the *Who?* and the *Why?* of such a program are certainly key, Zuse was looking more at how something like this could be possible. Although he was asking the right questions, the technology to test his theories was simply not available to him as it is to us now.

In recent years, new discoveries have directed scientists right back to Zuse's original questions. Picking up where he left off, a growing number are now thinking along the same lines and asking the same question: *Are we living in a virtual simulation?* If so, then the universe and everything in it is what and where it is because something in the cosmic program put it there. And that would mean that we're living in a digital reality where everything is made of *information* rather than *things*.

In 2006 Seth Lloyd, the designer of the first feasible quantum computer, took the idea of a digital universe one step further, elevating it from a question of *What if?* to the statement of *It is*. Based on his research in the new field of digital physics, he leaves little doubt as to where he stands in this emerging view of reality. "The history of the universe is, in effect, a huge and ongoing quantum computation," he asserts.[10] Just in case there's any uncertainty in our minds about precisely what Lloyd is saying here, he clarifies his findings. Rather than suggesting that the universe may be *like* a quantum computer, he blasts us into the most radical description of reality to emerge in the last 2,000 years, stating: "The universe *is* a quantum computer [my emphasis]."[11] From Lloyd's perspective, everything that exists is the output of the universe's computer. "As the computation proceeds, reality unfolds," he explains.[12]

> **Belief Code 6:**
>
> Just as we can run a simulated program that looks and feels real, studies suggest that the universe itself may be the output of a huge and ancient simulation—a computer program—that began long ago. If so, then to know the program's code is to know the rules of reality itself.

Wow! At first blush we find our minds reeling from the magnitude of what such a possibility implies. Then we find ourselves taking a closer look and a deeper breath, sitting back in our chairs, and saying, "Hmm . . . this actually makes sense. It makes *a lot* of sense. This may just be the way things really work!" The reason is because the comparison between the atoms of the everyday world and the information of a computer's works so well.

### Thinking of Atoms as Data

To begin such a comparison, let's take a look at what we know about computers. No matter how large or small, how simple or sophisticated, every computer has a language that it uses to get things done. In our familiar desk- or laptop, that language is a code based on patterns of numbers called *bits,* which is simply the computerese shorthand for the longer phrase "binary digits."

And "binary digits" simply means that all information is coded as patterns of 1's and 0's, "*ons*" and "*offs,*" the shorthand for the polarities that make the universe what it is. Because there are only two choices in polarity, the code of bits is called a *binary* language. In the most basic way of thinking of matter and energy, this represents everything: matter and non-matter, positive and negative, yes and no, male and female. In the case of the bits themselves, it's 1's and 0's, where 1 represents "on" and 0 represents "off." Binary code is just as simple as that.

But don't think that bits don't hold much power just because they're based on a simple idea. On the contrary: Binary language may be the *most* powerful in the universe. It represents the way things seem to be: They either are or they aren't. This language is universal. As amazing as it sounds, all computers—from those that guide our astronauts to the moon to the one in your car that tells you when it's time for an oil change—are based on a code made up of different combinations of 1's and 0's.

This code of bits is believed to be so universal that NASA even used it to inscribe the message that left Earth in 1972 aboard the *Pioneer 10* spacecraft. The idea was that if intelligent life ever found the football-sized probe, the binary language would tell them that we're a species that understands the way the universe works.

In 1983, *Pioneer 10* became the first artificial object from Earth to pass Pluto and leave our solar system. It was last heard from on January 22, 2003, when the sensors of the Deep Space Network picked up the final faint signal as the tiny craft hurtled deep into interstellar space. Although its power source has weakened over the last 35 years, scientists believe that *Pioneer 10* is still intact and on course, heading toward the star Aldebaran, where it should arrive in about two million years. When it does, it will be carrying a calling card from Earth in the universal language of binary numbers.

Just as every computer uses binary language to get things done, it looks as if the computer of the universe uses bits as well. Rather than being made of 1's and 0's, however, the bits of creation appear to be the stuff everything is made from: *atoms.* The atoms of our reality either exist as matter or they don't. They're either here or not here, "on" or "off."

In a recent interview, Seth Lloyd described a conversation that he had with his young daughter in which the irony of thinking of the universe as bits rather than as atoms became very clear. After Lloyd explained to his daughter how it's possible to program the universe, she replied, "No, Daddy, everything is made of atoms, except for light."[13]

From one perspective, she is absolutely correct. Lloyd acknowledged this, while offering yet another perspective. "Yes, Zoey," he agreed, "but those atoms are also information. You can think of atoms as carrying bits of information, or you can think of bits of information as carrying atoms. You can't separate the two."[14]

> **Belief Code 7:** When we think of the universe as a program, atoms represent "bits" of information that work just the way familiar computer bits do. They are either "on," as physical matter, or "off," as invisible waves.

### Question: What Is the Universe Computing?
### Answer: Itself

In another interview exploring consciousness as information and what it all may mean, Lloyd was asked the question that typically arises when we think of the universe as a computer: *If the entire universe, and everything in it, is really part of one great big quantum computer, then what is the purpose? What is the universe computing?*

Lloyd answered in a way that is reminiscent of something that we might expect to hear after trekking for weeks in the snow-covered peaks of the Himalayas searching for a great wise master hidden in a forgotten monastery. The simplicity of his response, and the magnitude of what it means, calls to mind the kind of answer we might find in just such a place: "[The universe] computes itself. It computes the flow of orange juice as you drink it, or the position of each atom in your cells. . . . But the vast majority of the universe's thinking is about humble vibrations and collisions of atoms."[15] At first, we may believe that one atom colliding with another doesn't really make all that much difference in our lives. After all, it happens all of the time, right? . . . Maybe. Or maybe not.

The implication of what Lloyd is saying invites us to think again. He reminds us how what he calls "the dance of matter and light" had the power to produce our universe and everything in it. His book *Computing the Universe* describes how the simple act of just the right atoms bumping into just the right other atoms can affect everything: "All interactions between particles in the universe convey not only energy but also information—in other words, particles not only collide, they compute. As the computation proceeds, reality unfolds."[16] From this way of thinking of things, we're the product of energy, movement, and matter touching matter—a big cosmic dance in the truest sense of the word.

In much the same way, John Wheeler was thinking about the universe as information in the 1980s. He explained, "Every *it*—every particle, every field of force, even the space-time continuum itself—derives its function, its meaning, its very existence entirely from binary choices, *bits*. What we call reality arises . . . from the posing of yes/no questions."[17] In other words, Wheeler was suggesting that the "things" that make the universe and life what they "are" are really information, little specks of polarity. Everything boils down to opposites: pluses and minuses, male and female, on and off.

### How Does Our Virtual Universe Work?

If, as Wheeler proposes, the particles of the universe are like computer bits of information and, as Lloyd states, "The universe is a quantum computer," then the question of what it *would* mean to know that everything is based upon a code has now changed to: *What does it mean?* As we'll see, the evidence suggests that the odds are greater than not that we're living in some kind of a simulated reality.

So now that we've opened the door to such a powerful possibility, let's continue with this line of thinking and take our possibilities yet one step further. In our simulated reality, do we have access to the code that makes all things possible? Can we upgrade the program of life, healing, peace, and everyday reality just in the way we can the code of our Internet connection or word processor? At the very least, such a possibility is intriguing.

From this perspective, for example, miracles are programs that bypass the "limits" of science, and the unfortunate accidents and bizarre occurrences that just seem to "happen" sometimes are due to occasional glitches in the computer's programs. Invariably, these questions open the door to even deeper ones—and with them, the mysteries that may not be answered anytime soon:

- Who is the programmer that started our cosmic computer simulation?

- Does the idea of a cosmic architect relate to our ideas of God?

- How long has the consciousness computer been running?

- What does the "beginning" and the "end" of time and life really mean?

- When we die, do we simply leave our simulation and continue existing in a realm outside of our virtual reality?

While these are all good questions, they are also beyond the scope of what we can do justice to in this book. There is an additional question, however, the answer to which may solve the mysteries of the others as well. It is simply this: *How does it all work?*

As stated earlier, we could study the creation of the universe and how it got here for another hundred years and still not have all of the answers. While such an investigation is certainly worthwhile, it may do little to address the urgent problems that face our world today. With the threat of global war and the very real chance that it will involve atomic weapons, the emergence of new disease from viruses that seem impervious to our arsenal of drugs, and the suffering brought on by drought and starvation that has already begun as the result of abrupt climate change, we simply don't have the luxury of another century to understand every iota of the universe's secrets before we act.

Clearly, now is the time to apply what we do know about the way our universe works in order to address the problems that threaten our survival and our future. And it all begins with our understanding of our cosmic belief code. When we master the language of that code, we can use it in our lives for everything from healing and reversing disease to successful relationships between people and peaceful cooperation among nations.

To think of the entire universe as an ongoing computer program, however, is huge! The idea seems so big and so complex that it could take forever just to know where we begin. A new branch of study may hold the clue. If so, we can start solving the mystery of the unknown by using the analogy of what we already do know. And it may all be much simpler than we thought possible.

### The Whole Universe from a Few Good Patterns

The science of the last 300 years has led to an inescapable conclusion about the reality of our everyday world: Everything is ultimately made of the same stuff. From the dust of distant stars to you and me, ultimately everything that "is" emerges from the vast soup of quantum energy (what "could be"). And without fail, when it does, it manifests as predictable patterns that follow the rules of nature.

Water is a perfect example. When two hydrogen atoms connect to one oxygen atom as a molecule of $H_2O$, the pattern of the bond between them is always identical. It always forms the same angle, which is always 104 degrees. The pattern is predictable. It is reliable—and because it is, water is always water.

It's all about the patterns.

So to pose the question of how the universe may work as a big computer, what we're really asking ourselves is how its energy creates patterns. This is where the boundary between our everyday world and the esoteric mysteries describing the universe becomes fuzzy.

When Zuse began to think of the universe as a computer, he was considering how it seemed to work like the one in his laboratory. The resemblance led him to suspect that not only were they similar in the way they operated, but also the way they processed information. He began to look for equivalent functions for his computer in the universe.

Reasoning that the bit is the smallest unit of information that a computer processes, he considered the atom—the smallest unit of matter that retains its elemental properties—as its equivalent. From this perspective, all that we can see, feel, and touch in the universe, then, is the matter made of the atoms that are in the "on" state. The ones that we don't see, those that exist in the invisible (virtual) state, are in the "off" position.

Just as the axiom "As above, so below; as below, so above" describes how the orbits of an electron can help us understand those of a solar system, Zuse's analogy offers a powerful metaphor that may go a long way toward doing the same thing for reality itself. It is simple. It is elegant. Perhaps most important, it works.

In a 1996 paper titled "A Computer Scientist's View of Life, the Universe, and Everything," Jürgen Schmidhuber of Dalle Molle Institute for Artificial Intelligence elaborated on Zuse's ideas.[18]

Exploring the possibility that our universe is the output of an ancient reality program that has been running for a very long time, Schmidhuber begins with the assumption that sometime in our distant past a great intelligence began the program that created "all possible universes." I have intentionally bypassed the complex equations that he uses to arrive at his conclusions and have cut to the portion that is relevant to what's under discussion.

Because his theory assumes that everything began at a moment in time with a fixed amount of information, he suggests, "Any universe's state at a given time is describable by a finite number of bits." His second assumption describes why this is important to us, as he concludes: "One of the many universes is ours."[19] In other words, Schmidhuber is suggesting that, just as it is with any simulation, the universe began with a certain amount of information—a certain number of atoms (bits)—which remains with us today and can be identified and accounted for. What a powerful and intriguing way to think about how the universe works! If in fact everything is really the information that Zuse, Schmidhuber, and others describe, then where do we fit in the universe's consciousness computer?

We've all heard the adage "When the student is ready, the teacher will appear." In much the same way, we find that when the idea is ready, the technology to explore it will materialize. It generally happens just in the nick of time. History shows that the right mathematical formula, the right experiments, and the right computer chip mysteriously arrive exactly when we need them to join the pieces of a new paradigm into something that becomes useful in our lives. The corollary to such new insights is that once they occur, there's no turning back.

This is precisely what's happening with the theories of the universe as a computer. While visionaries such as Zuse may have been thinking about it as long ago as the 1940s, in his day the mathematics to explore such radical ideas was simply not available. It wasn't until 30 years later that all of that changed. A new branch burst onto the scene, forever changing the way we think of everything from nature and our bodies, to wars and the stock market: fractal mathematics.

In the 1970s a professor at Yale University, Benoit Mandelbrot, developed a way for us to see the underlying structure that makes the world as it is. That structure is made of patterns—and more specifically, patterns within patterns within patterns . . . and so on. He called his new way of seeing things *fractal geometry,* or simply *fractals.*

Before Mandelbrot's discovery, mathematicians used euclidean geometry to describe the world. The belief was that nature itself was too complex for there to be a single formula that represents it accurately. For that reason, many of us have grown up learning a geometry that only approximates nature, using lines, squares, circles, and curves. We also know that it's impossible to represent a tree or a mountain range using what we learned. For precisely this reason, our first drawings of trees looked like lollipops on sticks.

Nature doesn't use perfect lines and curves to build trees, mountains, and clouds. Instead, it uses fragments that, when taken as a whole, become the mountains, clouds, and trees. In a fractal, each piece, no matter how tiny, resembles the larger pattern that it's a part of. When Mandelbrot programmed his simple formula into a computer, the output was stunning. By seeing everything in the natural world as small fragments that look a lot like other small fragments and combining them into larger patterns, the images that were produced did more than approximate nature.

© Florinc/Dreamstime

© Tupungato/Dreamstime

**Figure 1.** In the 1970s, Benoit Mandelbrot programmed a computer to produce the first fractal images like the one seen here on the left. Since that time, scientists have found that fractal geometry can mimic even the most complex patterns of nature, such as the fern leaf on the right. This discovery supports the possibility that nature and the universe may be the output of such patterns created by a huge quantum program that began long ago.

They looked *exactly* like nature. And that is precisely what Mandelbrot's new geometry was showing us about our world. Nature builds itself in patterns that are similar yet not identical. The term to describe this kind of similarity is *self-similarity*.

Seemingly overnight, it became possible to use fractals to replicate everything from the coastline of a continent to an exploding supernova. The key was to find the right formula—the right program. And this is the idea that brings us back to thinking of the universe as the output of an ancient and ongoing quantum program.

**Belief Code 8:**
Nature uses a few simple, self-similar, and repeating patterns—fractals—to build atoms into the familiar patterns of everything from elements and molecules to rocks, trees, and us.

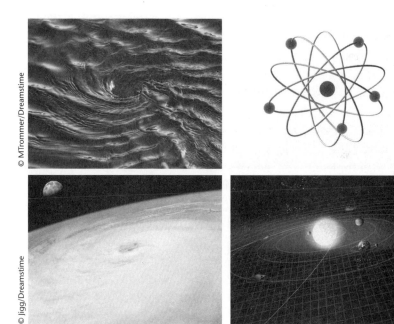

**Figure 2.** Examples of fractals in nature. The bottom image on the left is a NASA image showing the eye of a hurricane from space, and the image above it is a water vortex. The similarities are striking. The bottom image on the right is a graphic depiction of our solar system, and at top is a mechanical model of the atom. Both sets of images illustrate how self-similar, repeating patterns can be used to describe the universe from the very small to the very large, differing only in scale.

If the universe is the output of an unimaginably long-running computer program, then the computer must be producing the fractal patterns that we see as nature. For the first time, this new mathematics removes the stumbling block of *how* such a program may be possible. Instead of the electronic output of bits creating what we see on-screen, the consciousness computer of the universe uses atoms to produce rocks, trees, birds, plants, and even us.

### A Fractal Key to the Universe

A fractal view of the universe implies that everything from a single atom to the entire cosmos is made of just a few natural patterns. While they may combine, repeat, and build themselves on larger scales, even in their complexity they can still be reduced to a few simple forms.

The idea is certainly attractive; in fact, it's beautiful. Thinking of the universe as a fractal reality crosses the artificial separation that we have placed on our knowledge in the past, weaving very different disciplines of science and philosophy together into one great, elegant story of how the universe is constructed. The fractal view of the cosmos is so complete that it even accounts for the aesthetic qualities of balance and symmetry that artists, mathematicians, philosophers, and physicists aspire to in the highest forms of their crafts.

The universal appeal of this way of thinking certainly fulfills physicist John Wheeler's prophetic statement: "Surely someday . . . we will grasp the central idea of it all as so simple, so beautiful, so compelling that we will all say to each other, 'Oh, how could it have been otherwise!'"[20]

> **Belief Code 9:** If the universe is made of repeating patterns, then to understand something on a small scale provides a powerful window into similar forms on a grand scale.

In addition to accommodating the requirements of so many different ways of thinking, the fractal model of our universe has another important advantage: It holds the key to unlocking nothing less than the inner workings of the universe.

If our little desktop computers are based in fractal ideas that mimic the way the universe works, then when we learn about storing information on hard drives and performing downloads, we're really teaching ourselves how *reality* works. If so, we're ultimately gaining insight into nothing less than the mind of the great architect that set the universe into motion. So maybe the computer that we use to pass the time with a quick game of solitaire or e-mails to friends is much more than we have imagined. It may be that the compact technology on your desk actually holds the key to the greatest mystery in the universe.

### Big or Small, a Computer Is Always a Computer

While computers have gone through a tremendous evolution in size and speed since they burst on the scene in the mid-20th century, in some ways they have changed very little. Whether they fill an entire room or are miniaturized to fit into the palm of our hand, all computers have some things in common.

Regardless of its size, for example, a computer will always need hardware, an operating system, and programs to create its output. To shed new light on reality, however, it's important to understand just what these parts of a computer really do.

What follows is a brief explanation of each and the role it plays in an electronic computer. Although the descriptions themselves are tremendously oversimplified, they will allow us to compare the fractal of electronic computers to the larger workings of the universe. The parallels are fascinating. The similarity is unmistakable.

— The **output** of a computer is the result of the work it's done. All of the computations that happen inside the bits, chips, and circuits that compose its hardware are made visible as the information that we see as charts, graphs, words, and pictures. The output may be shown on a screen through a projector, printed on a piece of paper, displayed on a monitor, or all of the above.

— The **operating system** is the link between the hardware and the software. Through it, the input from our programs is translated into an even more complex language—the machine language—that speaks directly with the chips, memory, and storage of our computer. Whether it's the familiar Macintosh or Windows platforms or the specialized ones developed for specific tasks, the operating system is the reason why the commands we type into our keyboard make sense to the computer.

— The **programs** translate the commands that we've written in human language into a more complex one that will ultimately communicate with the processors of the computer itself. Examples include the familiar software such as Word, PowerPoint, Photoshop, and Excel that we install onto our computers to get things done.

While there are exotic forms of computers that are exceptions, by and large the three basic components in the preceding descriptions apply to nearly every computer in existence. When we apply these principles to the idea of the universe as a computer, *consciousness itself* becomes the operating system. Just as Microsoft's Windows or Apple's Macintosh operating systems are the link between our computer's input and its electronics, consciousness is what bridges *our* input with the stuff everything is made of.

It's a powerful analogy, and if our computers really mimic the way the universe works on a larger scale, it tells us two important things:

1. First, for all intents and purposes, the operating system of any computer is fixed. It doesn't change. In other words, it "is" what it is. So when we want our computer to do something different, we don't change the operating system—we change what goes into it.

2. This leads to the second important key to understanding how the universe works. To transform reality, we must alter the one thing that is not fixed: the programs themselves. For our universe, these are what we call "beliefs." So in this way of thinking of things, belief becomes the software (the *belief*-ware) that programs reality.

Summarizing the parallels between a familiar electronic computer and the universe, the following chart gives us a powerful clue as to how we may access the building blocks of the universe:

| Comparison Between an Electronic Computer and the Universe (as a Computer) | | |
|---|---|---|
| **Function** | **Electronic Computer** | **Universe Computer** |
| Basic Unit of Information | Bit | Atom |
| Output | Pictures, Charts, Words, Graphs, etc. | Reality |
| Operating System | Windows, Macintosh, Unix, etc. | Consciousness |
| Programs | Word, Excel, PowerPoint, etc. | Beliefs |

**Figure 3.** For both the universe (as a consciousness computer) and an electronic computer, the way to change the output is through the programs that the operating system recognizes.

Every day we offer the literal input of our belief-commands to the consciousness of the universe, which translates our personal and collective instructions into the reality of our health, the quality of our relationships, and the peace of our world. How to create the beliefs in our hearts that change the reality of our universe is a great secret, lost in the 4th century, from the most cherished Judeo-Christian traditions.

**Belief Code 10:** Belief is the "program" that creates patterns in reality.

The Gospel of Thomas offers a beautiful example of a powerful belief. In the pages of this controversial Gnostic text, identified as a rare record of Jesus's sayings, the master is describing the key to living in this world. He explains how the union of thought and emotion creates a power that can literally change our reality. "When you make the two one [thought and emotion]," he begins, "you will become the sons of man, and when you say, 'Mountain move away,' it will move away."[21]

The power of belief and of what we feel about our beliefs are also the crux of the wisdom preserved in the most magnificent, pristine, isolated, and remote locations remaining in the world today. From the high-altitude monasteries of the Tibetan plateau, Egypt's Sinai Peninsula, and the southern Andes Mountains of Peru, to the oral teaching of native peoples throughout the Americas, the power of human belief and how to hone it into a potent force in our lives has been preserved as a well-kept secret.

At this point you may be asking yourself the same question that I found myself wondering about as a senior computer systems designer working in the aerospace and defense industry more than 20 years ago: *If belief is so powerful, and if we all have this power within us, then why doesn't everyone know that we have it?* Why don't we all use it every day?

I found the answer where I'd least expected it: in the words of a young native guide leading a tour through an ancient village in the high desert of northern New Mexico.

### The Secret That Hides in Plain Sight

"The best way to hide something is to keep it in plain sight."

Those were the words that drifted across the dusty road leading into the Taos Pueblo on a hot afternoon in August of 1991. I'd set the day aside to explore the place that held such an attraction for some of the most inspirational creative figures of 20th century. From Ansel Adams and Georgia O'Keeffe, to D. H. Lawrence and Jim Morrison (from the rock group the Doors), the mystique and beauty of the high deserts has changed the lives of artists and their art.

I glanced in the direction of the voice to see where such a curious statement had originated. Across the road I saw a small tour group following a beautiful Native American man as he led them through the main plaza of the pueblo. As I stepped closer to hear what the young guide was saying, I quickly became part of the crowd that was shuffling toward the central part of the plaza. While we were walking, a woman in the group asked the guide about the spiritual beliefs of the Tewa people (the name that the original Taos natives called themselves based on the red willows that grow along the river).

"Do you still practice the old ways here, or do you keep those things hidden from outsiders?"

"'The old ways'?" our guide echoed. "You mean like old medicine? Are you asking if we still have a medicine man around here?"

Now the guide really had my attention. Five years earlier, I had walked into the same pueblo for the first time and had asked the very same question. I'd quickly discovered that the spiritual practices of the local people are a sensitive topic, something that isn't shared openly beyond close friends and tribal members. When such a question comes up, it's not unusual to find that the subject is either changed quickly or simply ignored altogether.

Today, however, neither happened. Instead, our guide offered a cryptic reply that left more of a lingering mystery than it offered answers. "No way!" he said, "We don't have medicine people here any longer. We're modern people living in the 20th century, with modern medicine." Then, as he looked directly into the eyes of the woman who had asked the question, he repeated the sentence that had drawn me to the group only moments before: "The best way to hide something is to keep it in plain sight."

As the words left his mouth, I could see the twinkle in his eye. He was letting her know that while "officially" the medicine people no longer practiced, their wisdom remained—safe, sound, and protected from the modern world.

Now it was my turn to ask a question. "I heard you say that earlier," I said. "Just what does it mean to hide something 'in plain sight'? How do you do that?"

"Just what I said," he replied. "Our ways are the ways of the land, of the earth. There is no secret to our medicine. When you understand who you are and your relationship to the land, you understand the medicine. The old ways are all around you, everywhere," he continued. "Here, I'll show you . . ."

Suddenly our guide turned around and began retracing his steps back toward the pueblo entrance we had just come from. Pointing to our left, he began walking toward a building that was unlike anything I'd ever seen before. As we left the road and walked along the side of an ancient-looking wall, I found myself staring at what looked like a cross between the thick buttresses of an old frontier fort and the unmistakable bell towers of a chapel—a Catholic chapel—that had been built 400 years before.

Our guide laughed at our surprise as he opened the gate and motioned us into the courtyard. It was old and beautiful. As I stood in front of the main entrance, I held my camera up to capture the brilliance of the deep blue New Mexico sky that surrounded the silhouette of the bells still hanging in the towers.

When Spanish conquerors first arrived in the pristine wilderness of northern New Mexico, they weren't prepared for what they found. Rather than the primitive tribes and temporary homes that they'd expected, they found an advanced civilization already in place. There were roads, multistory homes (jokingly called America's first condominiums by today's residents), passive solar heating and cooling, and a system of recycling that left virtually no waste from the entire population.

The early pueblo people practiced a powerful spirituality that allowed them to live in balance with the land for more than a millennium. All of that changed quickly, however, after the explorers came on the scene. "We already had a religion," our guide explained, "but it wasn't what the Spanish were looking for. It wasn't Christianity. Although our beliefs had many of the same ideas that you find in 'modern' religions, the Spanish didn't understand. They forced us to accept what they believed."

It was a difficult situation for the early pueblo residents. They weren't nomads who could simply pack everything and move to another valley. They had permanent homes that protected them from the hot desert summer and insulated them from the harsh winds of the high-altitude winter. They couldn't turn their backs on a thousand years of traditions that they believed in, nor could they honestly embrace the God of the Spanish explorers.

"The choice was clear," our guide continued. His ancestors had to conform to the religion of the explorers or lose everything. So they compromised. In a maneuver of sheer brilliance, they masked their beliefs, hiding them in the language and customs that satisfied the Spanish. In doing so, they kept their land, their culture, and their past intact.

I ran my fingers over the hammered studs that held the old wooden planks of the door in place. As we stepped inside the little chapel, the sounds of the bustling pueblo outside fell away. All that remained was the still, quiet air of this 400-year-old holy place. As I looked around the sanctuary, I saw images that were vaguely familiar, similar to those I'd seen in the great cathedrals of Peru and Bolivia, the icons of Christianity. But something was different here.

"The Spaniards called their creator 'God,'" our guide broke the silence. "While God was not quite the same as our creator, it was close enough, and we began to call our Great Spirit by the same name. The santos [saints] that the church recognized were like the spirits that we honor and call into our prayers. Mother Earth that brings us crops, rain, and life they called 'Mary.' We substituted their names for our beliefs." So that explained why this church looked a little different from those that I'd seen in the past. The outward symbols were masking a deeper spirituality and the true beliefs of another time.

Of course! I thought. That accounted for why the clothes of the female saints change colors throughout the year. They do so to match the seasons, with white in the winter, yellow in the spring, and so on. And that's why the images of "Father Sun" and "Mother Earth" peek out from behind the saints on the altar.

"See, I told you. Our traditions are still here, even after 400 years!" our guide said with a big grin on his face. His voice echoed through the empty space below the exposed timbers and vaulted ceiling. As he rounded the corner at the back of the room and walked toward me, he clarified what he meant. "For those who know the symbols, nothing was ever lost. We still change Mary's clothes to honor the seasons. We still bring flowers from the desert that holds the spirit of life. It's all here, hidden in plain sight for everyone to see."

I felt that I had gotten to know our guide a little better. I couldn't imagine what it must have been like for his people when everything changed four centuries ago. I had a renewed respect for the strength and courage, as well as the ingenuity, that they had to have had in order to mask their traditions with another religion. Now the mysterious words that I'd heard less than an hour before made sense. The best way to hide something is to place it where no one expects it to be: everywhere.

Like the people of the Taos Pueblo cloaking their spiritual beliefs in the traditions of modern religion, is it possible that we've masked a great secret as well? Could something as simple as our heartfelt belief really hold so much power that mystical traditions, the world's religions, and even entire nations were built around it? Just as native wisdom has been hidden in the plain sight of another tradition, have we done the same with what has been called the most powerful force in the universe? The answer to each of the questions is the same: *Yes!*

The difference between our secret and the hidden religion of the pueblo is that the native people have remembered what they placed into hiding four centuries ago. The question is: *Have we?* Or has something else happened? Have we concealed the power of belief from ourselves for so long that we've forgotten it while it remains in plain sight?

While there are many explanations as to *how* such powerful knowledge could have been lost for so long and *why* it was hidden to begin with, the first step in awakening the force of belief in our lives is to understand precisely what it is and how it works. When we do so, we give ourselves nothing less than the gift of speaking "quantum"—and programming the universe!

CHAPTER TWO

# Programming the Universe: The Science of Belief

. . . . . . . . . . . . . . . . . . . . . . . . . . . . . . . . . . . . . . . . . . .

*"The universe may be nothing more than
a giant hologram created by the mind."*
— **David Bohm** (1917–1992), physicist

*What seems to Be, Is,
to those to whom it seems to Be.*
— **William Blake** (1757–1827), poet

. . . . . . . . . . . . . . . . . . . . . . . . . . . . . . . . . . . . . . . . . . .

Just when we were getting comfortable with the "laws" of physics and biology and were convinced that we could master nature, everything changed. Suddenly we're told that atoms no longer look like tiny solar systems and DNA isn't quite the language that we thought it was, and now we find that it's impossible for us to simply observe our world without somehow affecting it.

In the words of Princeton University physicist John Wheeler, "We had this old idea, that there was a universe *out there* [my emphasis], and here is man, the observer, safely protected from the universe by a six-inch slab of plate glass."[1] Referring to the late-20th-century experiments that show us how simply looking at something actually changes what we're looking at, Wheeler continues, "Now we learn from the quantum world that even to observe so minuscule an object as an electron we have to shatter that plate glass; we have to reach in there. . . . So the old word *observer* simply has to be crossed off the books, and we must put in the new word *participator*."[2] In other words, the discoveries reveal that we are active contributors to everything that we see in the world around us, precisely as the spiritual traditions of the past have said that we are.

In light of such discoveries, we now find ourselves at a curious crossroads where we must sort out which of our beliefs about the world are true, which ones aren't, what works, and what doesn't. An interesting by-product of doing so is that this also gives us a new understanding of where and how science and spirituality fit into our lives.

With the foundation of what science once held sacred crumbling in so many respects and quantum physics telling us that when we watch something, we change what we're watching, the line between science and spirituality has become very fuzzy. And it's for that very reason that the scientific community has viewed the power of belief so skeptically.

When we talk about the power of "invisible forces" such as belief, to many scientists we've crossed the line that separates science from everything else. Maybe it's precisely because this line is so hard to define that we often learn about it only after we've already crossed it. My personal belief is that by relaxing the boundaries that have traditionally kept science and spirituality separate, we'll ultimately find the power of a greater wisdom. With the new discoveries showing that consciousness affects everything from the cells of our bodies to the atoms of our world, belief is clearly at the forefront of that exploration today. Interestingly, it has also become the place where science, faith, and even spirituality seem to be finding common ground.

## Beliefs That Change Our Bodies

When I was in school, I was taught that regardless of what I may think, feel, or believe, the world around me is unaffected. No matter how powerfully I was flooded with love, fear, anger, or compassion, I was told that the world would never be directly impacted by my inner experiences because they weren't really "real." Rather, they were just something mysteriously happening to me alone inside of my brain, and were insignificant in the overall scheme of the universe.

As noted previously, a new genre of scientific investigation has forever changed that view. The title of a 1998 study from the Weizmann Institute of Science in Rehovot, Israel, says it all: "Quantum Theory Demonstrated: Observation Affects Reality." In terms that sound more like a philosopher's hypothesis than a scientific conclusion, the paper describes how we affect reality just by watching it.[3] This powerful phenomenon has attracted the attention of innovators ranging from doctors and scientists to clergy and artists.

The results are clear. The implications are mind-boggling. The studies prove that rather than being buffered from our world and the things that make life what it is, we're intimately connected with everything from the cells of our bodies to the atoms of our world and beyond. Our experience of consciousness expressed as feeling and belief is doing the connecting. The act of us simply looking at our world—projecting the feelings and beliefs that we have as we focus our awareness on the particles that the universe is made of—changes those particles while we're looking.

With such discoveries in mind, it's natural to question what role this relationship between observation and reality has played in our everyday lives in the past. Have we already witnessed the effects of our observations and simply not recognized what we were seeing? Could our role as "participators" explain mysteries such as spontaneous remission of disease or miraculous healings? And, if so, what do these connections tell us about our own well-being?

✳

While the following situation itself is hypothetical, it's created as a composite from several true-life examples of something that doctors see on a routine basis yet are trained to dismiss because there's no "rational" explanation that accounts for healing without medicine. As we shall see, however, *there is a scientific reason,* and the same science that discounts these spontaneous healings as "miracles" actually gives us the mechanism that explains why they work.

In the make-believe lunchroom of a make-believe hospital some-where in a big city on the East Coast of the United States, two doctors are discussing a successful and mysterious healing that has occurred in one of their patients. It's *successful* because the patient's anomalous tissue growths on her legs have suddenly disappeared. It's *mysterious* because, while she was told that she was being administered a new treatment that would cure her condition, in reality all she received was tap water mixed with a colored dye.

She was part of a double-blind experiment where she and other patients with similar conditions were randomly selected and informed that a brand-new "breakthrough" treatment would be applied. Some received the real medicine, and some were simply given the colored water. *The key in this study is that all of the patients were told that by the time the treatment wore off, their condition would be healed.* In the case of the doctors' patient, the dye disappeared in 24 hours. When it did, her condition vanished as well.

Let's listen in as the doctors—one a skeptic and the other a believer in the power of belief—discuss the miracle over lunch.

**Believing Doctor:** What a great healing! What a fantastic way to end the morning. All we did was help the woman believe in her own recovery. When we did, her beliefs became the instructions that commanded her body, which then took over. It knew exactly what to do and healed itself.

**Skeptical Doctor:** Hold on a minute—not so fast. How do you *know* that it was the woman who healed herself? How do you *know* that it was her body that knew what to do? Maybe her condition was purely psychosomatic to begin with. If that was the case, we simply cured a psychological condition and healing the growths was a by-product.

**Believing Doctor:** Precisely. That's the whole point. The new studies are showing that many of the physical ailments that we treat are the result of psychological experiences—*subconscious beliefs that program the body.* The condition that we just treated was the expression of our patient's inner experience—*her beliefs.*

**Skeptical Doctor:** If that's true, then where does that leave us? Are we curing physical or psychological conditions?

**Believing Doctor:** Precisely!

**Skeptical Doctor:** Hmm . . . that changes everything! I think I liked it better when the patient was out of the picture and *we* were the ones doing the healing.

**Believing Doctor:** Now you've just missed the whole point. We were *never* doing the healing! It's just that now we acknowledge the *placebo* that's tricking the patients into reconnecting with their own belief-to-body relationship. They're still doing the healing.

**Skeptical Doctor:** Oh yeah . . . yeah . . . that's right . . . I knew that. . . .

Beliefs have long been known to have healing powers. The controversy centers around whether or not it's the belief itself that does the healing or if the experience of belief triggers a biological process that ultimately leads to the recovery. For the layperson, the distinction may sound like splitting hairs. While doctors can't explain precisely *why* some patients cure themselves through their beliefs, the effect has been documented so many times that at the very least we must accept that there *is* a correlation between the body's repairing itself and the patient's belief that the healing has taken place.

**Belief Code 11:**
What we *believe* to
be true in life may be
more powerful than what
others accept as truth.

*Healing Beliefs:*
*The Placebo Effect*

In 1955, H. K. Beecher, the chief of anesthesiology at Massachusetts General Hospital in Boston, published a landmark paper entitled "The Powerful Placebo."[4] In it, Beecher described his review of more than two dozen medical case histories and his findings, documenting that up to one-third of the patients healed from essentially nothing. The term used to describe this phenomenon was the *placebo response*—or, as it is more commonly known, the *placebo effect.*

The Latin word *placebo* was used in early Christian traditions as part of the ritual reading of Psalms 116:9. This passage begins with the words *Placebo Domino in regione vivorum,* which mean "I shall please the Lord in the land of the living."[5] Although there's some controversy regarding the Latin and the original Hebrew translation of the same phrase, the word *placebo* itself is unaffected and generally translated as "I will/shall please."

Today, *placebo* is used to describe any form of treatment where patients are led to believe that they're experiencing a beneficial procedure or receiving a curative agent, while in reality they're given something that has no known healing properties. The placebo can be as simple as a sugar pill or common saline solution or as complex as an actual surgery during which nothing is done. In other words, while the patients have agreed to participate in a medical study, they may not know precisely what their role in it will be. To test the placebo effect, they may undergo all of the experiences of surgery—including anesthesia, incisions, and sutures—while in reality nothing is added, taken away, or changed. No organs are treated. No tumors are removed.

What's important here is that the patients *believe* something is done. Based on their trust of the doctor and modern medicine, *they believe* that what they've experienced will help their condition. In the presence of their belief, their body responds *as if* they'd actually taken the drug or undergone a real procedure.

While Beecher reported that around one-third of the patients he reviewed responded positively to a placebo, other studies have placed the response rate even higher, depending on the condition for which patients were treated. Migraine headaches and wart removal, for example, have had high success rates. The following excerpt from an article published in *The New York Times* in 2000 reveals just how powerful the placebo effect can be:

> Forty years ago, a young Seattle cardiologist named Leonard Cobb conducted a unique trial of a procedure then commonly used for angina, in which doctors made small incisions in the chest and tied knots in two arteries to try to increase blood flow to the heart. It was a popular technique—90 percent of patients reported that it helped—but when Cobb compared it with placebo surgery in which he made incisions but did not tie off the arteries, the sham operations proved just as successful. The procedure, known as internal mammary ligation, was soon abandoned.[6]

In May 2004, a group of scientists at Italy's University of Turin Medical School conducted an unprecedented study investigating the power of belief to heal in a medical situation. It began with administering drugs that mimic dopamine and relieve patients' symptoms. It's important to note here that the drugs have a short life span in the body and their effects last only about 60 minutes. As they wear off, the symptoms return. Twenty-four hours later, the patients underwent a medical procedure where they *believed* that they would receive a substance to restore their brain chemistry to normal levels. In reality, however, they were given a simple saline solution that should have had no effect on their condition.

Following the procedure, electronic scans of the patients' brains showed something that's nothing short of a miracle. Their brain cells had responded to the procedure *as if* they'd been given the drug that originally eased their symptoms. Commenting on the remarkable nature of the study, the team's leader, Fabrizio Benedetti, stated, "It's the first time we've seen it [the effect] at the single neuron level."[7] The University of Turin findings supported studies that had been conducted earlier by a team at the University of British Columbia in Vancouver. In that investigation, it was reported that placebos could actually raise the brain levels of dopamine in the patients who receive them. Linking his studies to the earlier ones, Benedetti speculated that "the changes we ourselves observed are also induced by release of dopamine."[8]

It may be precisely *because* of this effect that William James, M.D., the man known as the "father" of psychology, never actually practiced the medicine that he was trained to offer. In an article written in 1864, he left little doubt as to why he suspected that the real power of healing was less about the procedures and more about the way doctors helped their patients feel about themselves: "My first impressions [about medicine] are that there is much humbug therein, and that, with the exception of surgery, in which something positive is sometimes accomplished, a doctor does more by the moral effect of his presence on the patient and family, than by anything else."[9]

For as long as there have been people, there have been attempts to alleviate their suffering and cure the medical conditions that they experience. While the history of healing can be traced back more than 8,000 years, "modern" medicine is considered to have begun only in the 20th century. Before that time, it's possible that many of the remedies used may have contained very little in the way of active ingredients. If this is true, then the placebo effect may actually account for a large percentage of past healings and may have played a key role in helping humankind survive into modern times.

If life-affirming beliefs do in fact have the power to reverse disease and heal our bodies, then we must ask ourselves an obvious question: *How much damage do negative beliefs carry?* How does the way we think about our age, for example, actually affect the way we grow older? What are the consequences of being bombarded with media messages that tell us we're sick rather than ones that celebrate our health? We need look no further than our friends, our family, and the world around us to find the answers to these questions.

Since the attacks on September 11, 2001, for example, we've been conditioned to believe that we live in a world where we aren't safe. It should come as no surprise, then, to learn that the general level of anxiety in the U.S., as well as anxiety-related issues of mental health, has increased during that same period of time. Studies in 2002 indicated that as many as 35 percent of the individuals exposed to the trauma of 9/11 could be at risk for developing post-traumatic stress disorder.[10] Five years later, that possibility became a reality when the high-school-aged children who initially experienced America's worst terrorist attack began showing an increased demand for anxiety-related treatment.

In March 2007, the Yale Medical Group reported on a study conducted by the Anxiety Disorders Association of America (ADAA). The paper documented that as the age-group who witnessed the attacks have matured, a "growing number of students [are] coming to college with a history of mental illness, with an increase after 9/11."[11] While intuitively we know that *positive beliefs* of safety and well-being are good for us, these statistics appear to be confirming what we already suspect: that while life-affirming beliefs can heal us, *negative beliefs* from shock and trauma can hurt us as well. Here the proof is, coming from a medical perspective.

In the preceding example, while the perceived danger may or may not be real, it's the students' belief that they live in an unsafe world that contributes to their stress. Constantly told that there's a general threat, yet without anything specific that they can do about it, they find themselves in the situation that affects so many in the U.S. today: the limbo state of "fight or flight," with nothing to confront and nowhere to go.

While the experts can argue to what degree an actual threat exists, the point here is that if we feel and believe that we're not safe, our bodies react as if the threat is real. While in our minds we may say, *Oh, it's a relatively safe world,* the fact is that we've been told by people of authority to "watch out." It's no surprise that our society has been a little "on edge" since September 2001.

*Dangerous Beliefs: The Nocebo Effect*

Just as the belief that we've been given a healing agent can promote our bodies' life-affirming chemistry, the reverse can happen if we believe that we're in a life-*threatening* situation. This is called the *nocebo effect.* A number of landmark studies have proven beyond any reasonable doubt that this effect is just as powerful as, but running in the opposite direction of, that of the placebo. According to Arthur Barsky, a psychiatrist at Boston's Brigham and Women's Hospital, it's the patients' expectation—the belief that a treatment either won't work for them or will have harmful side effects—that plays what he calls "a significant role in the outcome of the treatment."[12]

Even when patients are given a treatment that's proven useful in the past, if they believe it's of little or no value for them, that impression can have a powerfully negative effect. I remember reading about an experiment reported a few years ago on people who were having respiratory problems. (I also recall thinking, *I'm happy that I'm not one of those people being experimented on.*) In the tests, subjects who were known to have asthma were given a vapor that the researchers informed them was a chemical irritant. Although it was really only an atomized saline solution, almost half of the participants developed breathing problems, with some experiencing a full-blown asthma attack! When they were told that they were being treated with another, healing substance, they recovered immediately. In reality, however, the new treatment was only saline in water as well.

In their book *Honey, Mud, Maggots, and Other Medical Marvels: The Science Behind Folk Remedies and Old Wives' Tales,* Robert and Michèle Root-Bernstein summarize this unexpected effect, stating, "The nocebo effect can reverse the body's response to true medical treatment from positive to negative."[13]

Similar to the way physicists have discovered that the expectations of the observers during an experiment influence its outcome, a doctor stating, "Well, we'll *try* this treatment and see what it does . . . it *might* help a little" can make or break the treatment. It's for this very reason that even the slightest hint from a physician that a treatment may not work can have devastating consequences for its success. It can be so devastating, in fact, that it can kill. The famous Framingham Heart Study, initiated under the direction of the National Heart Institute (now known as the National Heart, Lung, and Blood Institute— NHLBI) in 1948, documented the power of just such an effect.[14]

The study began with 5,209 men and women, all from Framingham, Massachusetts, who were between the ages of 30 and 62. The purpose of the research was to follow a cross section of people over a long period of time to identify the then-unknown factors of heart disease. In 1971 the program initiated a second study based on the children of the original group, and the research has now begun to recruit a third group, composed of the grandchildren of the original subjects.

Every two years, the participants are evaluated for the risk factors that have been identified throughout the study. Although the study group represents a broad cross section of people from a variety of lifestyles, the discovery that the participants' belief played a role in their risk for heart disease was surprising to the researchers. Of the many statistics drawn from the study, correlations showed that women who *believed* they were prone to heart disease were nearly four times as likely to die as those with similar risk factors who didn't hold this belief.[15]

While medical science may not fully understand *why* the effect exists, it's clear beyond any reasonable doubt that there is a compelling link between what we *believe* about our bodies and the quality of life and healing that actually occurs. But does the effect stop there? Does the power of our belief end at the boundary defined by our bodies, or does it go further? If so, does that effect explain the things that we've called "miracles" in the past?

### Beliefs That Change Our World

While the theories of belief are interesting and the experiments can be convincing, when it comes to accepting the role that belief plays in our lives, my scientific training still likes to see something real—a meaningful application of what the theories describe.

As I mentioned in *The Divine Matrix,* one of the most powerful examples of group feeling and belief affecting a broad geographic area was documented as a daring experiment during the war between Lebanon and Israel that began in 1982. It was during that time that researchers trained a group of people to "feel" peace in their bodies while believing that it was already present within them, rather than simply thinking about it in their minds or praying "for" it to occur. For this particular experiment, those involved used a form of meditation known as TM (Transcendental Meditation) to achieve that feeling.

At appointed times on specific days of the month, these people were positioned throughout the war-torn areas of the Middle East. During the window of time when they were feeling peace, terrorist activities ceased, the rate of crimes against people went down, the number of emergency-room visits declined, and the incidence of traffic accidents dropped. When the participants' feelings changed, the statistics were reversed. This study confirmed the earlier findings: When a small percentage of the population achieved peace within themselves, it was reflected in the world around them.

The experiments took into account the days of the week, holidays, and even lunar cycles; and the data was so consistent that the researchers were able to identify how many people are needed to share the experience of peace before it's mirrored in their world. The number is the square root of one percent of the population. This formula produces figures that are smaller than we might expect. For example, in a city of one million people, the number is about 100. In a world of 6 billion, it's just under 8,000. This calculation represents only the minimum needed to begin the process. The more people involved in feeling peace, the faster the effect is created. The study became known as the International Peace Project in the Middle East, and the results were eventually published in *The Journal of Conflict Resolution* in 1988.[16]

While these and similar studies obviously deserve more exploration, they show that there's an effect here that's beyond chance. The quality of our innermost beliefs clearly influences that of our outer world. From this perspective, everything from the healing of our bodies to the peace between nations; from our success in business, relationships, and careers to the failure of marriages and the breakup of families . . . all must be considered as reflections of us and of the meaning that we give to the experiences of our lives.

Historically, to suggest that what we believe in our hearts and minds can somehow have any effect whatsoever on our bodies is a very different way of seeing things, a real s-t-r-e-t-c-h. And even to many of those comfortable with the mind/body relationship, implying that our beliefs can affect the world beyond our physical selves is simply out of the question. For others, however, it's right up their alley.

For those who have been raised with a holistic view of the world, the universal power of belief is completely aligned with what they have always known. For everyone, however, it offers the ability to change the pain, suffering, war, and lack in life—and to do so by choice.

In what may be one of the greatest—and, to some, perhaps the most bizarre—of ironies, there is one condition that must be met before we can unleash the power of belief: *We must believe in belief itself for it to have power in our lives.* This very condition sometimes makes it difficult to give this subject serious consideration.

While miraculous healings are possible and "synchronicities" abound in our lives, we must be open to them and willing to accept them in order to receive their benefits. In other words, *we need a reason* to believe in them. That's where the distinction between belief, faith, and science comes in.

> **Belief Code 12:**
> We must accept the power of belief to tap it in our lives.

### Belief, Faith, and Science

Today we are at a pivotal time when three major ways of knowing —belief, faith, and science—are being tested against the reality of our world. When we're asked how we know that something is true, we generally rely upon assumptions that come from one, or some combination, of these ways of seeing the world to answer.

While science distinguishes itself through the obvious characteristics of facts and proof, differentiating between belief and faith sometimes isn't so clear. In fact, people often use these two words interchangeably. Maybe the best way to make the distinction that's so important for this book is through an example.

If I have a history of running marathons, and someone asks me whether I can complete one in the near future, my answer would be yes. It would be based on the *fact* of my having completed marathons in the past, and my belief that I could do so again at some point in the future. There's no reason to suspect differently. So in this example, I can say that I *believe* in my ability to finish the race, and my belief is based on the evidence of direct experience.

Now let's say that I receive a packet from the marathon sponsors in the mail a week later and discover an important piece of information that they neglected to tell me originally. Suddenly I discover that the finish line for the marathon is at the top of Pikes Peak in Colorado Springs, Colorado, at 14,000-plus feet above sea level. Now I'm in a different situation.

While it's true that I *have* run the 26.2-mile-long races in the past, and I *have* completed them successfully, what is also true is that I've never run one at such a high altitude. So now I don't have the evidence that I can finish this marathon successfully. Although I have no reason to believe that I can't, I've simply never done it before, so I have to speculate about my success. My speculation is based in *faith,* because I have no direct evidence to support my success.

While this may seem like a silly example, it illustrates the difference between faith and belief. Belief is based on evidence. While our faith in something *may* have evidence as well, the key here is that it doesn't have to. To a person of faith, it's unnecessary.

We often hear of the distinction between faith and belief within a religious context. For some people God's existence, for example, is true without question. They proclaim that they need no proof and simply have faith that the Almighty is present. For others, however, in what they feel is the absence of direct evidence of God, they find it difficult to accept His existence as a fact. While they might like to and may even spend their lives searching for what they consider to be that validation, it may not appear in the form they expect. So for these people, evidence of God is elusive, and they can't allow themselves to believe without it.

At the same time, though, the search for the Divine leads other people to see the order and beauty that science has revealed in everything from the smallest particles of matter to the most distant galaxies as undeniable proof of an intelligent universe. For them, science itself has proven God's existence.

Interestingly, in modern times, *faith* and *belief* are used so interchangeably that even the *Merriam-Webster Online Dictionary* uses the words to define one another. The word *faith* has its roots in the Latin *fidere,* meaning "to trust." It's defined as "firm belief in something for which there is no proof."[17] The same dictionary identifies *belief* as a synonym for *faith,* yet defines it with a very important distinction. *Belief* is "conviction of the truth of some statement or the reality of some being or phenomenon *especially when based on examination of evidence* [my italics]."[18]

As I mentioned earlier, it's the facts that set science apart from faith or belief. Although they can change, and often do as new conditions are discovered, the definition of *science* is widely accepted as "knowledge or a system of knowledge covering general truths or the operation of general laws especially as obtained and tested through scientific method."[19]

In every sense of this definition, exploring our power of belief as a consistent, repeatable, and learnable experience is a science. In other words, if we go about it in a certain way and believe in a certain way, we can expect a certain outcome. By adopting this manner of thinking about belief, we can consider it a science.

To unlock the mystery of belief as a science may be one of the most pivotal discoveries that we could make in the modern age. With it, we may find that we've given ourselves the power to change the conditions of pain and suffering that have ravaged our world for as long as anyone can remember.

The key here is to find out how to make sense of our beliefs. We must discover a way to think of them within a framework of something that we already know and that's easy to explain—something like a computer. If we can conceptualize belief as the program of consciousness, then we can do just that.

In Chapter 1, we explored the possibility that the universe itself may operate like a massive computer, with beliefs as its programs. We already know how a computer works. And we already know how its programs work. So the framework for such a comparison is already in place. Now, let's take our exploration one step further . . . to the next level. Let's see precisely how much of a program our beliefs really are and how we can create new belief-programs that speak to the computer of the universe.

---

**Belief Code 13:**
Belief is defined as the certainty that comes from accepting what we *think is true* in our minds, coupled with what we *feel is true* in our hearts.

---

### *Belief* Defined

The reasons why something as simple as belief holds such power could fill volumes. This book is written as a place to begin. In the last section, belief was described as being more than faith without facts. It goes beyond simple agreement and compromise. For the purposes of this book, we'll define *belief* as "an experience that happens in both our minds and our bodies." Specifically, we can say that it's "the acceptance that comes from what we think is true in our minds married with what we feel is true in our hearts."

Belief is a universal experience that we may understand, share, and develop as a potent agent of change. The following points lay the foundation for a description of what belief is and how we may use ours as a powerful inner technology.

— **Belief is a language.** And it's not just *any* language. Both ancient traditions and modern science describe belief as the key to the very "stuff" that makes our universe. With no words or outward expression, therefore, the seemingly powerless experience that we call "belief" is *the* language that touches the quantum stuff of our bodies and our world. In the presence of our deepest beliefs, the limits of biology, physics, time, and space that we know today become a thing of the past.

— **Belief is a personal experience.** Everyone has beliefs. Each individual's experience of them is different. There are no right or wrong ways to believe, and there's nothing that we should or shouldn't do. There are no secret ancient postures to hold with our bodies and no sacred positioning of our fingers and hands. If there were, then the power of belief would be limited only to those with full access to the functioning of their bodies and limbs.

Likewise, belief is more than what we think in our minds. It's more than what a book, a ritual, a practice, or the research of another person tells us is true. Belief is *our acceptance* of what we have witnessed, experienced, or know for ourselves.

— **Belief is personal power.** Our beliefs hold all of the power we need for all of the change we choose: the power to send healing commands to our immune systems, stem cells, and DNA; to bring an end to violence in our homes and communities or in entire geographic areas; and to heal our deepest hurts, breathe life into our greatest joys, and literally create our everyday Reality (with a capital *R*). Through our beliefs we hold the gift of the single most powerful force in the universe: the ability to change our lives, our bodies, and our world by choice.

To grasp the power of beliefs, we need to understand them on a nuts-and-bolts level: precisely how they're formed and where they reside in the body. While they're closely associated with feelings, they fall into a category that works a little differently from simple anger or joy. When we identify this subtle yet powerful difference, it becomes clear how we may change our beliefs when they no longer serve us.

### The Anatomy of Belief

For our beliefs to have an effect on the world around us, two things must be in place:

1. First, there must be something that our beliefs travel through—a medium—to carry our inner experiences beyond our bodies.

2. Second, our beliefs must have the power to do something in the physical world. In other words, they must rearrange the atoms that the universe is composed of to make something happen.

Beyond any reasonable doubt, the new discoveries show that our beliefs possess both of these attributes.

Both scientific discoveries and spiritual principles acknowledge that the space between the world and us (which we may have thought of as empty in the past)—regardless of what we call it or how it's defined—is anything *but* empty. Early in the 20th century, Albert Einstein made reference to the mysterious force that he was certain exists in the space that fills what we see as the universe around us. "Nature shows us only the tail of the lion," he stated, suggesting that there's something more to what we see as reality, even if we can't glimpse it from our particular cosmic vantage point. With a beauty and eloquence that's typical of Einstein's view of the universe, he elaborated on his analogy of the cosmos: "I do not doubt that the lion belongs to it [the tail] even though he cannot at once reveal himself because of his enormous size."[20]

As described in Chapter 1, the new discoveries show that Einstein's lion is the force that physicist Max Planck described as the matrix that fills empty space and connects everything with everything else. This matrix provides the conduit between our inner experiences of belief and the world that surrounds us. Today, modern science has refined our understanding of Planck's matrix, describing it as a form of energy that is already everywhere at every moment and has existed since time began with the big bang.

The existence of this field implies two things that directly affect the power of belief in our lives. While these principles may contradict many well-established tenets of science and spirituality, they also open the door to an empowering way of seeing our world and living our lives.

1. The first principle suggests that because everything exists *within* the Divine Matrix, everything is connected. If things are connected, then, what we do in one place must influence what is happening in other places. The influence may be huge or it may be small, depending upon a number of factors that we address in this book. The key is that our inner experience in one place has the power to affect the world in another place. This power includes producing physical effects.

2. The second principle suggests that the Divine Matrix is holographic, meaning that any portion of the field contains everything in the field. This means that when we sit in our living room and *believe* in the healing of a loved one halfway around the world *as if it already exists,* the essence of our belief is already at its destination. In other words, the changes that we initiate within ourselves are already present everywhere, as a blueprint in the matrix. So our job is less about getting our good wishes to where another person may be located, and more about breathing life into the possibilities that we create as our beliefs.

"Okay," you're saying, "so there's a field of energy that holds everything together and we're part of that field. While it may make intuitive sense that everything is connected through this field, the fact that it is there still doesn't explain precisely *how* this connection works."

This is where the scientific discoveries of the last 100 years show us *why* our beliefs about the world can actually have any effect upon the world. Belief's effects are based in patterns of energy—the same energy that everything is made of. When we reduce the everyday world to patterns of this energy, suddenly our power to change reality not only makes sense, but it makes *a lot* of sense.

### Belief-Waves: Speaking the Language of Atoms

What follows is a flowchart that describes the general connection between energy, the atoms of reality, and belief. This will become the outline for us to explore each item in more detail and then to pull it all together in a way that's useful in our lives.

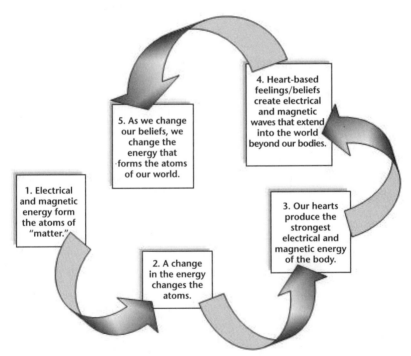

**Figure 4.** A flowchart diagramming the relationship between our beliefs and the changes they create in the physical world.

Clearly, science doesn't have all of the answers regarding precisely *how* our beliefs affect reality. If it did, we'd obviously be living in a very different world. What science *does* tell us for certain, however, is that our hearts are quite literally at the core of the electrical and magnetic fields that communicate with the organs within us. Studies also show that our heart fields aren't limited to the inside of our bodies. In fact, they have been measured to extend for distances as great as eight feet *beyond* the body.[21]

When I asked the heart researchers why the field of an organ as powerful as the human heart would be limited to only eight feet, they told me that the number was the result of a limitation in their equipment to measure such a field. In all probability, they confided, it extends for distances of miles beyond the place where the physical heart resides.

In 1993, a paper published by the Institute of HeartMath documented the fact that the information coded in our emotions plays a key role in the way the heart tells the brain which chemicals (things such as hormones, endorphins, and immune enhancers) to produce in the body at any given time.[22] More precisely, our emotions tell our brains *what we believe we need* in the moment. This effect of heart/brain communication is well documented in the open literature and generally accepted in the progressive medical community.

What is not so well recorded, however, is exactly how our beliefs can change our physical world. We may well come to find that this apparent "disconnect" in heart/belief/reality is a direct result of the life sciences lagging behind the most exciting discoveries of our day—discoveries that have invalidated the principles on which those disciplines were based.

There's a hierarchy of understanding that all science must conform to, and it's simply this: When one branch of science is based on the assumptions of another and the underlying science changes, everything that relies upon that foundational science must change as well. For example, we know that chemistry has a foundation in physics. We also know that biology is based on the principles of chemistry, which are grounded in physics, and so on. With this hierarchy in mind, let's look at where we find ourselves today in terms of scientific understanding.

From the time of Isaac Newton until the early 20th century, the scientific view of our world was a mechanical one based on "things" and their relationships with other "things." All that changed in 1925 with the acceptance of a quantum view of the universe. Suddenly, we began to think of the universe as fields of energy that exist as probabilities rather than a machine that's absolutely predictable.

The important thing here is that when the laws of physics changed, all of the scientific practices that relied on them should have done so as well. Some did. Mathematics changed. Chemistry changed. But biology and the life sciences didn't. So today many life scientists find themselves still working and teaching based on a mechanical view of things, rather than seeing the universe, the world, and our bodies as fields that are engaged in a perpetual dance of energy interacting with other energy. Thanks to the pioneering research of scientists such as Dr. Bruce Lipton, and his book *The Biology of Belief,* this situation is changing.

### The Language of Atoms

While scientists struggle to understand how beliefs affect our world through the traditional models of life and reality, the new view of everything as energy interacting with energy leaves us wondering how it could be any different. When we begin to see things from this perspective, it blows the doors right off of the limitations of our past. Suddenly, the mechanism that allows beliefs to change our physical world becomes clear. And it all begins with the way we think of matter itself.

If you haven't been in a classroom for a while or haven't read a book based in the "new physics," the revised thinking on what an atom looks like may surprise you. Rather than the mechanical model of things orbiting around other things—like a miniature solar system—the quantum atom is based on the probability that energy may be concentrated in one place or another at a given moment in time (Figure 5). What's important here is that the energy is made in part of the electrical and magnetic fields—*the same fields that we create in the thoughts of our brains and the beliefs of our hearts.* In other words, the universal experiences that we know as feeling and belief are the names that we give to the body's ability to convert our experiences into electrical and magnetic waves.

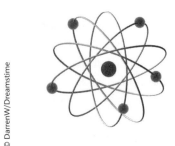 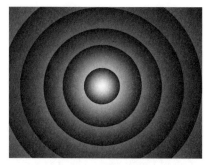

© DarrenW/Dreamstime

**Figure 5.** Illustration showing the old mechanical model of the atom as "things" (on the left) and the new quantum model of the atom as concentrations of energy in zones (on the right).

This is where things get really interesting. When either the electrical *or* the magnetic fields of an atom change—*or both do*—the atom changes: It alters the way it behaves, as well as the way it expresses itself as matter. And when the atom changes, so does our world.

The shifting of an atom's energy by a magnetic field is a well-documented phenomenon that was first recognized in 1896. Named after its discoverer, Nobel Prize laureate Pieter Zeeman, the *Zeeman effect* states that in the presence of magnetic force, the stuff that constitutes matter is transformed. In words that are clear and direct, classic-physics texts state, "When placed in an external magnetic field the energy of the atom changes . . . "[23]

A similar phenomenon, known as the *Stark effect* after its 1913 discoverer, Johannes Stark, is documented as taking place with electrical fields, which do electrically what the Zeeman effect does magnetically.[24] While both the Zeeman and the Stark effects are interesting individually, together they become the key to understanding the power of heart-based belief.

Studies by the Institute of HeartMath have shown that the electrical strength of the heart's signal, measured by an electrocardiogram

(EKG), is up to 60 times as great as the electrical signal from the human brain, measured by an electroencephalogram (EEG), while the heart's magnetic field is as much as 5,000 times stronger than that of the brain.[25] What's important here is that either field has the power to change the energy of atoms, *and we create both* in our experience of belief!

When we form heart-centered beliefs within our bodies, in the language of physics we're creating the electrical and magnetic expression of them as waves of energy, which aren't confined to our hearts or limited by the physical barrier of our skin and bones. So clearly we're "speaking" to the world around us in each moment of every day through a language that has no words: the belief-waves of our hearts.

In addition to pumping the blood of life *within* our bodies, we may think of the heart as a belief-to-matter translator. It converts the perceptions of our experiences, beliefs, and imagination into the coded language of waves that communicates with the world *beyond* our bodies. Perhaps this is what philosopher and poet John Mackenzie meant when he stated, "The distinction between what is real and what is imaginary is not one that can be finely maintained . . . all existing things are . . . imaginary."[26]

> **Belief Code 14:**
> Belief is expressed in the heart, where our experiences are translated into the electrical and magnetic waves that interact with the physical world.

So what does all of this mean? The bottom line is simple. The implications are profound.

The precise fields of energy that alter our world are created by the mysterious organ that holds our deepest beliefs. Perhaps it's no coincidence that the power to change our bodies and the atoms of matter is focused in the one place that's long been associated with the spiritual qualities that make us who we are: the heart. Truly, we can feel justified when we look to ourselves, then to one another, and from the place of deepest gratitude for all that we've experienced in life, simply say, "Bless our hearts!"

### *The Great Secret That Everyone Knows—Except Us!*

Through media phenomena such as the films and books *The Secret* and *What the Bleep Do We Know!?* the subject of how we use "thought" has become a hot topic of the day. Interestingly, however, the related experiences of feeling and emotion become almost secondary in the same discussions and sometimes are discounted altogether. When they are addressed, it's not uncommon to find that *feeling* and *emotion* are used interchangeably, lumped together as a nebulous experience that's kind of fuzzy and hard to define.

My mom and I have had this conversation many times over the years. "I always thought that feeling and emotion were the same thing," she has said to me on more occasions than I can count. It's not surprising that people make such generalizations. With few exceptions, science and spirituality—the two sources of knowledge that we've historically trusted to describe our world—both appear to have left the power of feeling and emotion completely out of the equation of life.

In our traditional version of the modern Bible, for instance, perhaps it's only a coincidence that the documents instructing us on the power of thought and emotion, such as the Gnostic Gospel of Thomas, are among the same ones that were "lost" during the biblical edits of the 4th century. While these references may be missing from the most cherished Judeo-Christian teachings, this isn't the case for other spiritual traditions.

As a scientist working in the defense industry in the mid-1980s, I thought that I'd find the best-preserved examples of these teachings in the places least disturbed by modern civilization. From the monasteries of Egypt's Gebel Musa and the Andes Mountains of Peru to the highlands of central China and Tibet, I found myself in some of the most remote and isolated sanctuaries remaining on Earth today, in search of precisely such teachings. It was on a clear, cold morning in 1998 that I heard the actual words describing the power of feeling in our lives in a way that couldn't be mistaken.

Each day on the Tibetan plateau is both summer and winter—summer in the direct high-altitude sun and winter as the rays disappear behind the jagged peaks of the Himalayas. It felt as if there was nothing between my skin and the ancient stones as I sat on the cold floor beneath me. But I knew I couldn't leave. This day was the reason why I'd invited a small group to join me in a journey that had led us halfway around the world.

For 14 days we'd acclimated our bodies to altitudes of up to 16,000 feet above sea level. Holding on to our seats, and even on to one another, we'd braced ourselves as our vintage bus crept over washed-away bridges and crawled through roadless desert, just to be in this very place in this precise moment—an 800-year-old monastery hidden at the base of the mountain.

I focused my attention directly into the eyes of the beautiful and timeless-looking man seated lotus-style in front of me, the abbot of the monastery. Through our translator, I'd just asked him the same question that I'd posed to each monk and nun we'd met throughout our pilgrimage. "When we see your prayers," I began, "what are you really *doing?* When we see you tone and chant for 14 and 16 hours a day . . . when we see the bells, the bowls, the gongs, the chimes, the mudras, and the mantras on the outside, *what is happening to you on the inside?*"

As the translator shared the abbot's reply, a powerful sensation rippled through my body, and I knew that this was the reason why we'd come to this place. "You have never seen our prayers," he answered, "because a prayer cannot be seen." Adjusting his heavy wool robes, the abbot continued: "What you have seen is what we do to create the feeling in our bodies. *Feeling is the prayer.*"

The clarity of the abbot's answer sent me reeling! His words echoed the ideas that had been recorded in ancient Gnostic and Christian traditions more than 2,000 years ago. In early translations of the biblical book of John (16:24, for example), we're invited to empower our prayers by *being* surrounded with (that is, feeling) our desires fulfilled, just as the abbot suggested: "Ask without hidden motive and *be surrounded by your answer.*" For our prayers to be answered, we must transcend the doubt that often accompanies the positive nature of our desire. Following a brief teaching on the power of overcoming our uncertainty, the Gnostic Gospel of Thomas preserves Jesus's precise instructions describing how to create the feelings that produce miracles.

In the mid-20th century, these words were discovered as part of Egypt's Nag Hammadi library. In no fewer than two different places we're given similar instructions and are invited to merge our thoughts and emotions into a single potent force. In verse 48, for example, we're told, "If two [thought and emotion] make peace with each other in this one house, they will say to the mountain, 'Move away' and it will move away."[27]

Verse 106 is strikingly similar, reiterating, "When you make the two one . . . when you say, 'Mountain move away!' it will move away."[28]

If the instructions have remained so consistent that the abbot was repeating the essence of a 2,000-year-old teaching, then it may still be useful to us today. Using nearly identical language, both the abbot and the scrolls were describing a form of prayer and a great secret that has been largely forgotten in the West. Belief and the feelings that we have about it are the language of miracles.

### Emotion, Thought, and Feeling: Separate yet Related Experiences

If we can truly grasp what our heart-based power of belief tells us about our world, then life takes on an entirely new meaning. We become architects of reality, rather than victims of mysterious forces that we can't see and don't understand. To do so, however, we must understand not only *how* our beliefs speak to the universe, but also *how* we may revise the conversation by changing them. When we accomplish this, we are truly programming the universe. And it all begins with understanding the three separate yet related experiences that we know as thought, feeling, and emotion.

The diagram in Figure 6 is from an ancient mystical text written in Sanskrit. It illustrates how we may use thought and emotion to create heart-based feelings and beliefs within our body. The key in this drawing is the location of the body's energy centers, known as *chakras* (a Sanskrit term meaning "spinning wheels of energy"). In the Sanskrit system, a distinction is made between the first three from the top of the head down, and the bottom three from the base of the spine upward. The role that these groups of chakras play in the creation of our beliefs is the key to taking charge of our lives.

When we understand the relationship between our thoughts, feelings, and emotions, we also recognize how our beliefs have the power to affect the world. While on a physical level each energy center is linked to one of the organs of the endocrine system, on an energetic level the chakras play different roles in our lives. In the following sections, we'll define *emotion, thought,* and *feeling* separately and then illustrate how they come together to form the inner experiences that become our reality.

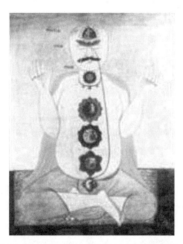

**Figure 6.** Illustration showing the concentration of the seven energy centers that form the chakra system running vertically from the crown to the perineum of the human body. This drawing comes from an ancient Sanskrit manuscript.

### *Emotion* Defined

The lower three chakras of creativity are commonly associated with our experience of emotion. When we think of these centers as pure energy, they represent the only two basic emotions that we're capable of in life: love and whatever we think of as its opposite. As strange as this may sound at first blush, as we'll see below, this definition shows that the joy, hate, and peace that we may have thought of as emotions in the past are, in fact, the *feelings* that result from the use of them.

We've all had experiences of love in our lives. And because *we're* all unique, these experiences have been as well. So when we talk about love's opposite, it can mean different things for different people. For some, it's the experience of fear; for others, it may be that of hate. Regardless of what we call it, however, when we get right down to the bare essence of the deepest teachings, love and its opposite are really two aspects of the same thing, two polarities of the same force: emotion.

Emotion is the power source that drives us forward in life. Love or fear is the driving force that propels us through the walls of resistance and catapults us beyond the barriers that keep us from our goals, dreams, and desires. Just as the power of any engine needs to be harnessed for it to be useful, the power of emotion must be channeled and focused for it to serve us in our lives. When we don't have clear direction, our emotions can become scattered and chaotic. We've all known the drama and chaos that often accompanies people who deal with life purely on this basis.

While these two emotions are a source of power in our lives, clearly this can be a mixed blessing. Our emotions can serve us, or they can destroy us. Which experience we have is determined by our ability to harness them and give them direction. And that's where the power of thought comes in.

### *Thought* Defined

Thoughts are associated with the upper three energy centers of our body—the chakras related to logic and communication. Whereas emotion can be considered a power source, thoughts are the guidance system that directs it, focusing it in precise ways. So while our thoughts are important, they have little power by themselves. In engineering terms, they may be considered scalar energy (a potential force) surrounding a *possible* situation, rather than the vector energy (an actual force) of something that's real and happening in our lives. This safety buffer prevents every passing thought in our minds from manifesting in reality. As the following statistics suggest, that's a really good thing.

A few years ago the National Science Foundation reported that the average person has somewhere in the neighborhood of 1,000 thoughts an hour. Depending on whether or not we could be considered "deep thinkers," we can have between 12,000 and 50,000 thoughts each day. Out of curiosity, sometimes I ask friends and co-workers to share what they're thinking. When I do, I quickly discover that many of their thoughts are about things that they would prefer to keep to themselves! Fortunately for us, most of our passing thoughts remain just that: brief glimpses into what could be, what might come to be, or what has been.

### *Feeling* Defined

A thought without the emotion to fuel it is just a thought—it isn't good, bad, right, or wrong. By itself, it has little effect on anything and is the imagining of a possibility that remains in the mind: the seed of what could be, suspended in time—harmless, and relatively powerless.

We call a thought without the emotional fuel that would bring it to life a *wish*. While possibly well intentioned, our wishes probably have little effect on our bodies or the world—until we awaken them.

As Figure 7 illustrates, when we marry the thoughts in our minds with the power of the emotions that emanate from our lower energy centers, we create *feelings*. Thus, a feeling is the union of what we think with the fuel of our love or fear for our thought. And now we have a definition for feelings and a way to understand how they're different from emotions.

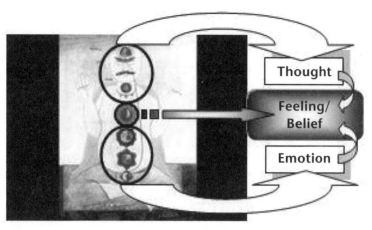

**Figure 7.** When we marry thoughts with the emotion of our love or fear regarding them, we create feelings. *Feelings* are defined as "the union of thought and emotion." They're the basis of our beliefs and are formed in our hearts.

Of course, while there are only two basic emotions—love and fear—we can experience an infinite number of feelings. Examples are anger, compassion, rage, jealousy, gratitude, disbelief, and peace, to name only a few. In engineering terms, they are a vector form of energy. In other words, they are where the action is and can really get things done! Our feelings can change the world.

### Belief: A Special Kind of Feeling

Belief is a form of feeling. When we hold a belief about something, we usually have a feeling—and often a strong one—about it. Any doubt about the truth of this statement disappears quickly when we ask people to share their feelings on topics with moral roots that ignite their deepest beliefs.

The death penalty, stem-cell research, whether to teach creationism or evolution in the classroom, abortion, and assisted suicide are all examples of topics that draw from us strong feelings as to their rightness or wrongness. While we may not always be aware of our true position on such subjects, the intensity of our emotional response when they come up in conversation is a good indicator of where we stand regarding the most hotly debated issues of our time. In one way or another, our feelings are based in what we believe.

To describe what sets belief apart from our everyday anger, compassion, and sadness, for example, let's take a closer look at how those feelings are created.

> **Belief Code 15:**
> Beliefs, and the feelings that we have about them, are the language that "speaks" to the quantum stuff that makes our reality.

### Honoring the Vibe

We defined *feeling* as the result of thoughts that are fueled by one of only two possible emotions: love or fear. What makes belief a special case is that it sometimes seems to happen *without* any thoughts—at least without any that we're consciously aware of.

We've all experienced a belief that just seems to "happen" and comes out of nowhere, such as a conviction that we're in the wrong place at the wrong time. While there may be no obvious reasons for it, we just know that it's definitely there. And it's usually in our best interest to honor our beliefs in the moment we have them. Later, in a safe environment, we can look back and explore what may have caused our "inner alarm" to sound. When we do, it's not uncommon to find that our beliefs have been sparked by something *beyond* the emotions of love or fear that create our typical feelings. That something is the power of what many people simply call the vibes of *body truth, body resonance,* or just plain *resonance.*

In its simplest form, *resonance* is an exchange of energy between two things. It's a two-way experience, allowing each "something" to come into balance with the other. Resonance plays a huge role in our lives in everything from tuning our televisions and radios to our favorite station, to the unforgettable feeling that we have when another human looks directly into our eyes and says, "I love you." Our experience of what we believe is all about resonance between us and the facts with which we're being confronted.

To get a clear idea of what resonance is, let's look at the example of shared vibration between two guitars placed on opposite sides of the same room. As the lowest string of either guitar is plucked, *the same string on the second instrument will vibrate* as if it were the one that was just plucked. Even though it's on the other side of the room and no one has physically touched it, it's still responding to the first guitar, because they're equal in their ability to share a particular kind of energy. In this case, the energy is in the form of a wave traveling through space and across the room.

And this is the same way we experience belief in our lives.

Rather than two guitars in a room tuned to match one another, we're beings of energy with the capacity to tune our bodies and share particular kinds of energy. When our thoughts direct our attention to a sight that we see, words that are spoken, or something that we otherwise experience in some way, our physical selves respond to the energy of that experience. When it resonates *with* us, we have a body-centered response that tells us that what we have seen or heard is "true"—at least it is for us in that moment. This is what makes body truth so interesting.

Whether or not the information or experience is *factual* isn't what this kind of truth is all about. The person experiencing resonance *believes* that it's true. And, in that moment, it *is* true for him or her. The individual's past experience, perceptions, judgments, and conditioning shape the experience into what he or she feels in the moment.

Equally interesting is the fact that the same person can face a similar situation a week later and find that it no longer resonates with him or her. Because it doesn't, it's no longer true. This happens because the individual's filters of perception have changed and the person simply no longer believes as he or she did a week earlier.

In their experience of body truth, people often have physical sensations that tell them they're resonating with what they've just experienced. Goose bumps; ringing of the ears; and a visible flushing of the face, upper chest, and arms are common expressions of body truth.

### Resonance in Action

Resonance is a two-way experience. In addition to telling us when something is true for us, it's also a defense mechanism that alerts us when we may be in a potentially harmful situation. When we find ourselves in the proverbial "dark alley," for example, we may actually feel as though we are in the wrong place at the wrong time. Our bodies "know" this; and the resulting symptoms can range from a mild, general weakness in the body, as if something is suddenly siphoning off all of our energy, to an extreme when the experience or information is so shocking to us that we break out in a cold sweat, with our face turning pasty white as our blood rushes away, preparing us for fight or flight.

Interestingly, we often have the same responses in the presence of lies, or at least information that our bodies *feel* is untrue. While it may be that we simply don't have all the facts, or that those we do have are perceived incorrectly, the key here is that in the instant we suspect a lie, we're responding to our experience of that moment. When we hear someone tell us something that we absolutely know beyond a shadow of a doubt is untrue, we feel a tension in our body that is commonly called our "bullsh*t detector."

While it may not always be based on facts that are knowable in the moment, our gut reaction to what others share with us can be an invaluable tool in situations that range from suspected infidelity in a romantic relationship, to reading a label on our favorite package of cookies that tells us that the additives and fats we're about to eat are "harmless."

My family recently had this experience when the "tree doctors" showed up at our door one day to spray our yard with a pesticide that would protect the neighborhood from certain insects. While they were telling us that the chemical was "harmless" to animals and humans, and even to children (whom I've always thought of as humans as well), we were also instructed to keep our pets, kids, and bare feet off of the lawn for 24 hours and to wipe everyone's shoes before coming into the house.

Although I'd done no research on the pesticide or the company and had no reason to doubt the man standing in front of me, who sincerely believed what his employer had told him, I knew in the core of my being that what I was being told was incorrect. The first words out of my mouth were to the effect that "if the chemical is really so 'safe,' then why all the precautions?"

After doing some quick investigating on the Internet, my suspicions were confirmed. The pesticide that was proposed was the same stuff that has been linked to a variety of health conditions, none of which were good. It's almost as if the company believes that as long as their product doesn't cause three-headed ants to appear in the yard a week later, the stuff is okay to use!

The key here is that we don't have to think about our experiences to determine if they're right for us. The body already knows the answers, and it responds with signals with which we're all familiar. And these are the experiences that tell us when we accept something as truthful in our lives and when we don't. The question is: *Do we have the wisdom or the courage to listen?*

### *Looking Before We Leap*

Sometimes we can use our gut feelings to tell us about the rightness or the wrongness of an experience *before* we actually have it. This is the beauty of being able to think about something ahead of time. In our minds we can model it and check it out from every angle to search for the pros and cons while it's still only a possibility. Scientists believe that we are the only form of life that uses our thinking abilities to reason in this way. This may be precisely why our ability to think about our beliefs is such a resilient part of our nature.

In a 2004 paper, Rebecca Saxe, Ph.D., assistant professor in the Department of Brain and Cognitive Sciences at the Massachusetts Institute of Technology (MIT), reported that the ability to apply reasoning to the things we believe "develops earlier and resists degradation longer than other, similarly structured kinds of logical reasoning."[29]

When we consider thought, feeling, and emotion as the way we simulate a situation before we actually confront it, we open the door to a powerful way of using these separate yet related experiences. By determining precisely *whether* we love or fear the things that we imagine, we also choose if and when our creations will ever come to life. In other words, our minds are just like simulators, and it's our thoughts that are doing the simulating. They allow us play out a given situation, and all of the possibilities that it may hold, before it ever happens. A big part of our situation preview is that we get to explore the outcome and the consequences of our actions before we ever act.

When I worked at corporations as an engineer, I had a friend who used his thoughts in this way when it came to where a romantic relationship might lead. I'm not saying that he did so consciously. During the times when I watched the process, it appeared that his relationship imaginings had been going on for so long that they were habitual and unconscious. I was fascinated by how he would play out scenarios in his mind, and the predicaments that he would find himself in as a result.

Within minutes of meeting a potential new romantic interest, for example, in his mind he would imagine what their relationship would be like and where it could lead. While everyone may do this to a degree, he carried *his* possibilities to the extreme.

During a lunch break, at a seminar or conference, or sometimes in the checkout line at the grocery store, he might meet a woman whom he felt powerfully attracted to. When he would begin to share such a story, I knew him well enough to anticipate what was coming next. Following their initial meeting, the next few moments would go something like this:

He would exchange a few words with the new acquaintance, and suddenly his mind was racing into the future, exploring all the possibilities of what life with this woman would be like. Maybe they would date for a year or so and then get married. And not long after, they could begin a family—that is, unless the new consulting business that they would start together kept them on the road so much that they wouldn't have time for one. But then, at their age, how long could they realistically travel with such frequency? So maybe they should just adopt and take trips with a nanny. And on it would go . . .

I'd listen to my friend's speculation about the possibilities of what could be, until he'd suddenly snap out of his daydream, look at me a little sheepishly, and realize that, in his mind, he had just described an entire lifetime with a woman whom he'd known for less than 20 minutes! The point of this story is that if every one of my friend's thoughts became the reality of his life, things would become very strange, very quickly. While we all use our ability to think about potential scenarios and logical outcomes, hopefully we do so more consciously and with much less intensity than my engineer friend.

### Thoughts, Wishes, Affirmations, and Prayers

The experience of affirmations is a perfect example of how the power of thought works. I've known people who used them every day of their lives—scribbled on sticky notes that were stuck to their bathroom mirrors, covering their car dashboards, and framing their computer screens at work. They would repeat the words hundreds and sometimes thousands of times each day, muttering such things as: "My perfect mate is manifesting for me now," or "I am abundant now and in all past, present, and future manifestations." Occasionally I'd ask them about their practice and if their affirmations really worked. Sometimes they did. Often they didn't.

When my friends' affirmations seemed to fail, I'd ask them why. What did they believe was the reason for the failure? There was a common thread that connected each explanation. For each instance that the affirmations didn't appear to work, the person using them was doing little more than simply reciting the words—*there was no emotion underlying them*. We've got to fuel our affirmation with the power of our love, as if it's already accomplished, for the new condition to become real in our lives. And this, I believe, is the key to a successful affirmation and what sets one apart from a wish and an empty thought.

## Thoughts and Wishes

As noted previously, a thought is simply the image in our minds of what's possible or what could become so in any given situation, from relationships and healing to everything in between. Without the energy of the love or fear that fuels our thought, it has little power and remains just what it is. In the case of the healings described earlier in this chapter, the idea of what a person's recovery would be like and how his or her life would change is an example of a thought. While where the healing begins is important, the thought alone is not enough to instigate it.

The desire or hope for a thought to come alive, without the emotion to give it that life, is a *wish*—it's simply the image of what is possible. In the absence of the emotion needed to bring it into the world of reality, a wish is open-ended. It can last for seconds, years, or an entire lifetime as the vision of what could be, suspended in time.

**Example:** Simply hoping, wishing, or saying that a healing is successful may have little effect upon the actual situation. In these experiences, we haven't yet arrived at the belief—the certainty that comes from acceptance of what we *think is true,* coupled with what we *feel is true* in our body—that makes the wish a reality.

### Affirmations and Prayers

A thought that's imbued with the power of emotion produces the feeling that brings it to life. When this happens, we've created an affirmation as well as a prayer. Both are based in feeling—and more precisely, in feeling as if the outcome has already happened. Studies have shown that the clearer and more specific we are, the greater the opportunity for a successful result.

This is why the abbot's words reminding us that "feeling is the prayer" are so powerful. They are taken from a lineage of teachings that has remained consistent and true for more than 5,000 years.

**Example:** A successful affirmation or prayer of healing would be based in feeling *from* the completed outcome. It's as if the healing has already happened. Through gratitude for what has already occurred, we create the changes in life that mirror our feeling.

### Belief: The Programs of Consciousness

"All that you behold, tho' it appears Without, it is Within, / In your Imagination, of which this World of Mortality is but a Shadow."[30] With these verses, the poet William Blake reminds us of the power living within each of us in every moment of every day. Although the words have changed, the similarity between what Blake is communicating and what the Buddhist traditions were telling us centuries ago is unmistakable.

If, as they state, "Reality exists only where the mind creates a focus" and all that we experience, "tho' it appears Without, it is Within," then clearly our beliefs are the programs that determine our experience.

Living in the 19th and early 20th centuries, William James was one of the most influential people of his time. A Renaissance man in the modern era, he was very clear regarding his view of the role that consciousness and belief play in our lives, even before he became a psychologist. In his 1904 paper "Does 'Consciousness' Exist?" he states that sometimes what we experience in consciousness is intangible and "figures as a thought."[31] At other times, however, he says that it figures as a "thing," becoming real in our lives. When the latter happens, he suggests that it's our power of belief that creates the actual fact.

While I've defined *belief* and given examples of how it works, it remains one of the most elusive of our experiences. And for that reason, it may also be one of the most difficult places to make a change. When we really believe something, we have a feeling about it. While we may call this an instinct or a gut reaction, the key to change is that our belief registers with us on a deep, perhaps even primal, level. While we don't have to understand belief to experience it, we do have to know how it works if we're to harness its power in our lives.

If we think of belief as the code that programs the universe, and if the little programs in our lives are really miniature examples (fractals) of the bigger ones of the universe, then understanding how a computer program is made should also explain how beliefs are formed. So let's begin by exploring our own as if they were simple programs. When we do, the nebulous idea of belief takes on a shape and form we can work with! We can see precisely how our inner experiences affect the outer world. Perhaps more important, we can also discover what to do more or less of to translate our hearts' desires into the reality of our lives.

While it may sound redundant to say that the purpose of a computer program is to get things done, it's important to state this clearly as we begin to think of *belief* as a program. If we're going to create a brand-new belief or change an existing one, we must be absolutely certain about what it is that we hope to accomplish. A fuzzy belief will undoubtedly give us a fuzzy result.

Programs can be complex or simple. Some literally contain millions of lines of computer code, and others can be as short as three simple statements. Regardless of their size, however, all programs have the same basic parts, which can be thought of as the commands that launch the program *(begin),* instruct it what to do *(work),* and tell it that the work is finished *(completion).*

Before an actual program is written, computer programmers often outline what they hope to accomplish in broad terms. Because it's not the true program itself, this is often called a *pseudo program.* Just as an outline for a school paper describes the highlights of the content and provides a map for the ideas that will be explored, the pseudo program identifies the key elements that the program will accomplish.

Because our goal is to use what we already know about electronic programs to understand those of consciousness, let's look at thought, feeling, and emotion as equivalent parts of that software. In Figure 8, we can see how our inner experiences perform the same role in consciousness as their counterparts do in our computers.

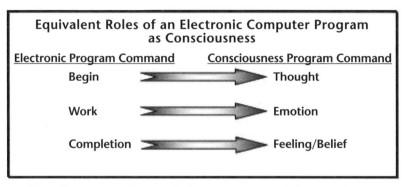

Figure 8. Comparison between the three generic elements for computer programs and their equivalents in the consciousness programs of the universe.

## The *Begin* Command

In an electronic computer, the begin command is what starts a program and gets things going. It's a specialized statement that provides all of the information that the program needs to do its work, including such things as the value given to certain symbols and how many times the computer will perform a task. When we create a belief in our consciousness computer, thought is the equivalent of a begin command.

With our thoughts, we can bring together everything we need to explore an experience before we actually have it. When considering whether or not to enter into a new relationship, for example, we can collect all of the information that will help us make our decision. If it's a romantic partnership, we can acknowledge the attributes of the other person and his or her life dreams, goals, and desires to see if our paths are compatible. We can ask questions about where and how the other person would like to live and where they place the priorities of career and children in their lives.

This gathering of information and assigning of values is like the begin command in our electronic computer. Just as we need all of the ingredients for a really good meal before we can prepare it, this is a necessary step before our belief program can begin.

## The *Work* Commands

The work commands tell the program what to do. They give meaning to the information that the begin command has identified, bringing it together in a useful, and meaningful, way. Emotion is the equivalent of the work commands.

Our love or fear for the things that we call to mind is what gives life to them. In the preceding example of romance, it's probably safe to assume that love is the emotion—the work command—that fuels our thoughts about our partner. It's our love for the possibilities that the new relationship brings to our lives that defines the feelings and beliefs that we experience. The dreams, goals, and desires that we have in common with our new partner or our loving aspirations for the person's dreams set into motion the events that become the reality of our lives.

## The *Completion* Command

Within the context of our consciousness program, the completion command is the beginning, rather than an end, of the process. It signals the point where all of the pieces have come together and our belief *in its finished form* can now become the template in our lives to express what we have created inside ourselves. Because our hearts convert our completed beliefs into the waves that carry information throughout our bodies and into the world, what we believe becomes the language that "speaks" to the quantum stuff that the universe is made of. Feeling is the equivalent of a completion command.

Just to be clear, this is not the kind of "completion" that brings everything to a grinding halt. In fact, the completion of our belief program does just the opposite: It signals that our building of a new belief is done so that the finished outcome can now manifest and become real. In the example we've been using, this is the equivalent of feeling as if the relationship is already in place, as if we've already embarked upon our new journey with our partner.

With these equivalents in mind, it's now easy to think of feeling and belief as the programs of consciousness. Because we're the ones creating them, that makes us the programmers. *We* choose which thoughts become our begin commands and which emotion signals that we're ready to bring them to life. Through inner technology of belief-ware, we're clearly the architects of our lives.

It all begins with what happens in the mysterious realm that we call the mind, that place where our experiences converge into the lasting record of a moment in time.

### CHAPTER THREE

# From Brain to Mind:
# Who's Running Our Belief Factory?

*"Our subconscious minds have no sense of humor,
play no jokes, and cannot tell the difference between
reality and an imagined thought or image."*
— **Robert Collier** (1885–1950), motivational author

*"The distinction between what is real and
what is imaginary is not one that can be finely
maintained . . . all existing things are . . . imaginary."*
— **John S. Mackenzie** (1860–1935), philosopher

In the previous chapters we've seen how the principles of a modern computer can help us understand consciousness. New studies show that the same analogy can also go a long way toward demystifying the relationship between the brain and the mind. In his groundbreaking book *Consciousness Explained,* Daniel Dennett, codirector of the Center for Cognitive Studies at Tufts University, says that we can actually think of the brain "as a computer of sorts," and that doing so gives us a powerful metaphor to understand how we use information.[1] Dennett's comparisons give us just what we need to navigate what he calls the *"terra incognita,"* or the unknown land, between what science tells us *about* our brains and what we experience *through* them.

The man commonly referred to as the "father" of the modern computer, mathematician John von Neumann, once calculated that the human brain could store as much as 280 quintillion bits of memory (that's 280 with 18 zeros following it). Not only can the brain store such an amazing amount of data, it can process it more quickly than any of today's fastest computers.[2] This is important because it's the way we gather, process, and store the information of life that determines our beliefs and where they come from.

Studies during the 1970s revealed that the memories of our experiences aren't limited to a specific place within the brain. The revolutionary work of neuroscientist Karl Pribram, for example, has shown that brain functions are more global than were once thought. Before Pribram's research, it was believed that there was a one-to-one correspondence between certain kinds of memory, conscious and subconscious, and the places where those memories are stored.

The problem was that the theory didn't pan out in laboratory tests. The experiments showed that animals kept their memories and continued their lives even though the parts of their brains that were believed to be responsible for such functions were removed. In other words, there wasn't a direct link between the memories and a physical place in the brain. It was obvious that the mechanical view of brain and memory wasn't the answer. Something else was happening— something that turned out to be both mysterious and wonderful.

During his research, Pribram noticed a similarity between the way in which the brain stores memories and another kind of information storage developed in the mid-20th century through patterns called *holograms.* If you were to ask someone to explain a hologram, he or she would probably begin by describing it as a special kind of photograph where the image on a surface suddenly appears three-dimensional when exposed to direct light. The process that creates these images involves a way of using laser light so that the picture becomes distributed over the entire surface of the film. It's this property of "distributedness" that makes the holographic film different from that of a typical camera.

In this way, every part of the surface contains the entire image just as it was originally seen, only on a smaller scale. And this is the definition of a hologram. It's a process that allows every part of "something" to contain the entire something. Nature is holographic and uses this principle to share information and make significant changes—such as healing mutations in DNA—quickly.

So whether we divide the universe into galaxies, humans into atoms, or memories into fragments, the principle is the same: Each piece mirrors the whole, only on a smaller scale. This is both the beauty and the power of the hologram—its information is *every*where and can be measured *any*where.

In the 1940s, scientist Dennis Gabor used complicated equations known as *Fourier transforms* to create the first holograms—work for which he was awarded a Nobel Prize in 1971. Pribram guessed that if the brain really works like a hologram and distributes information throughout its soft circuits, then it should process information in the same way Fourier's equations do. Knowing that the brain's cells create electrical waves, Pribram was able to test the patterns from brain circuits using the Fourier equations. Sure enough, his theory was correct. The experiments proved that the brain processes information in a way that's equivalent to a hologram.

Pribram clarified his model of the brain through the simple metaphor of holograms working within other holograms. In an interview, he explained, "The holograms within the visual system are . . . patch holograms."[3] These are smaller portions of a larger image. "The total image is composed much as it is in an insect eye that has hundreds of little lenses instead of one single big lens . . . You get the total pattern all woven together as a unified piece by the time you experience it."[4] This radically new way of thinking of ourselves, and the universe, gives nothing less than direct access to every possibility that we could ever wish or pray for, dream of, or imagine.

It all begins with our beliefs and the thoughts that contribute to them. While the beliefs themselves are formed in our hearts, as we saw in the last chapter, the thoughts that they come from originate in one of the two mysterious realms of our brain: the *conscious* or *subconscious mind.*

*Conscious and Subconscious Mind:*
*The Pilot and Autopilot*

While we obviously have one brain, we know that different parts of it work differently. The most commonly recognized distinction in the way the brain operates is our experience of the conscious mind and the subconscious mind. We've long known that both play a role in making *us* who we are. Now, new discoveries show us that they're also largely responsible for making *reality* what it is.

Our success and happiness; our failures and suffering; our physical conditions, such as infertility and immune disorders; and even our life expectancy have all been linked to our subconscious beliefs. And sometimes the most damaging ones begin early on, as we allow the experiences of other people to become the template for our own. To understand just how these connections between life and memory are made, and how we can change them, we need to understand the difference between our conscious and subconscious minds and how they work.

The conscious mind is the brain function that we generally feel most connected with, because it's the one that we're most aware of. It's the place where we create the image of ourselves that we see from the inside looking out, as well as what we want other people to see from the outside looking in. Through our conscious minds, we take in information about our day-to-day world: the people around us, what time it is, where we're going, and how we'll get there. We analyze and process all of that information and then make plans for what we'll do once we get where we're headed.

The experience of standing on the street corner of a busy intersection is a beautiful example of how the conscious mind works and how easy it is for the *sub*conscious one to take over. Consciously, we know that it's best for us to wait for the light on the other side of the street to signal when it's safe to cross. We also know that there are other people who won't pause and will chance the traffic before the light says that it's okay to walk, even at the risk of their own lives! While we might see others doing so, if *we* choose to wait for the "Walk" signal, our conscious mind has taken all of the factors into account and made that choice.

If, however, the crowd of people waiting on the corner with us collectively dart across the street because there's a break in the traffic and we simply "go with the flow" and move along with them while we're talking to a friend on our cell phone, then something else has happened. Because our attention was on the call, we weren't focused on the traffic light. We followed the others like the proverbial sheep because our subconscious mind made that choice. And the subconscious doesn't "think" about things—it simply reacts.

From this brief example, it's obvious that the subconscious mind plays a very different role than our conscious mind. For one thing, we're less aware of it—unless we're trained to recognize its language and the way it works, we may be completely oblivious to the fact that it's there at all. Using our computer analogy, we can think of the subconscious mind as the hard drive in the brain, doing what hard drives do: store a lot of information.

In fact, *your* subconscious mind has a record of everything that you've ever experienced during your entire lifetime. Not only does it hold a record of the events themselves, it also keeps a cross-referenced log of how you felt and what you believed about each one. That's right . . . every thought, every emotion, all of the accolades and encouragement you've ever received—as well as all of the harsh words, criticism, and betrayals—are stored right there on the hard drive of your subconscious mind.

And it's those experiences that unexpectedly surface in our lives, seemingly at the times when we would least like for them to be there!

### Question: When Does the Subconscious Mind Rest?
### Answer: Never

"Okay," you may be saying to yourself, "conscious or subconscious beliefs, holographic memories or not, let's say that all of the events of my life really *are* stored somewhere. Why do I care about my past experiences? Are they even important to me now?"

You bet they are! Here's why: The subconscious mind is much larger and more powerful than the conscious one. Although individual experiences may vary, the estimates are that upwards of 90 percent of our daily lives are directed from the subconscious level. Because this includes the functions that keep us alive each day, for the most part these automatic responses are a good thing.

Have you ever wondered what life would be like if your subconscious mind *wasn't* working at this level? What if you had to remind yourself, for example, when it was time to breathe in and when it was time to breathe out? Or what if you had to stop whatever you were doing after a really great meal and say to your body, *Okay, body, I'm finished with my meal now. Please begin the digestion process.*

> **Belief Code 16:**
> The subconscious mind is larger and faster than the conscious mind, and can account for as much as 90 percent of our activity each day.

For the biological functions that keep us alive every day, the subconscious mind is a great friend that does things automatically so that we can focus our attention on other things in life, such as love, passion, chocolate, and sunsets. The way in which the conscious and subconscious minds work and process the massive quantity of information both take in is what makes such a big difference to *us* and gives belief a central role in our lives.

While the conscious mind processes tremendous amounts of information, it does so relatively slowly, one piece of data at a time, just like the serial processor of a computer. Our subconscious mind, on the other hand, works like a computer's parallel processor: It divides information into smaller pieces that are sent to various places so that they can all be processed at the same time.

According to some estimates, the difference in the processing speeds of our conscious and subconscious minds is on the order of many magnitudes. Cell biologist Bruce Lipton, Ph.D., for example, describes the conscious mind as operating with the computer-processing power at about 40 bits of information per second, while the subconscious processes information at 20 *million* bits per second.[5]

In other words, the subconscious is 500,000 times faster at what it does. It may be precisely because of this difference that psychologist William James said that the power to move the world is in the subconscious mind. It's fast and works instinctively, without our thoughts and considerations getting in the way and slowing it down.

The ability to react rapidly and instinctively can be a good thing when we must make quick decisions. If we see a truck heading directly for us, for example, and it's a really big one, moving really fast, our subconscious mind reacts with everything it needs to get us out of the way. It doesn't wait while our conscious mind analyzes the situation with questions such as: *Yes, it's a truck, but what __kind__?* or *Just __how fast__ is that big truck coming toward me moving?*

If we waited for the slower, conscious mind to complete this kind of analysis, it might be too late to act. The point is that in situations that require a split-second decision, sometimes the details just aren't important. And that's where our subconscious does what it was built to do so very well: It acts *much* faster than the thinking mind. At other times, however, we pay the price for dealing with life from such a quick and reactive place—especially when our reactions are based on the beliefs of other people that we learned to mimic early in life.

### *Where Do Subconscious Beliefs Come From?*

Studies have shown that until the age of seven, our brains are in a hypnogogic or dreamlike state, where the mind is absorbing everything it can about our surroundings. During this time, we're literally like little sponges, spending our days soaking up information about the world around us with no filters to tell us what's appropriate and what's not. To us, it's all just information, and we record and store every bit of it.

This includes the things that we later recognize as the good, the bad, and the ugly—the judgments, biases, likes and dislikes, and behavior patterns of those around us, especially our primary caretakers. It may be precisely because of this impressionable state of mind that the founder of the Jesuit order, Ignatius of Loyola, stated, "Give me a child until he is 7, and I will give you the man."[6]

In terms that are nonscientific by today's standards, Loyola apparently knew the power of the subconscious mind, and that if he could instill the religious values of the Jesuits into the heads of young males, these convictions would be the basis of the beliefs they would have as adults. No doubt William James also had this very principle in mind when he said, "Could the young but realize how soon they will become mere walking bundles of habits, they would give more heed to their conduct while in the plastic state."[7]

Whether we're in a Jesuit school or our family home, we're immersed in the experiences of others at an age when we simply "download" them without any filtering of and discernment for what we're taking in. So it's not surprising that the beliefs of others become the foundation of what we hold true about the world and ourselves. In the very place where we formulate our beliefs, we have a record of every perspective that we were ever exposed to early in life—from every instance we were told that we could be whatever we set our minds to, to all of the times we were told that we'd never amount to anything. It's easy to see why the viewpoints of others become our beliefs.

> **Belief Code 17:**
> Many of our most deeply held beliefs are subconscious and begin when our brain state allows us to absorb the ideas of others before the age of seven.

Sometimes childhood beliefs stay with us for our entire lives, and sometimes we find good reasons to change them. We've all had the experience of believing that our parents were all-knowing and infallible when it came to the things that they told us, right? There was a period in my life when I thought my mother and father knew everything. It wasn't until I began comparing what I'd been taught with what other kids my age and their families believed that I discovered there were many ways to think of the world. Some of them were far different from what I'd learned growing up in a small town in America's conservative heartland.

### Memories and the Subconscious

Memory is a curious thing. Sometimes the details of the most important events of life fade within days, while the mundane moments become the memories that stay with us the longest.

I remember sitting on the shore of a river with my mother one day. It was autumn, the air was crisp, and I was bundled in layers of blankets to stay warm. Together we were watching groups of men rowing long, narrow boats quickly through the water. I remember the rhythm—it was perfect, the motion was smooth, and it seemed as if there wasn't a ripple in the water as the boats shot past us.

Similarly, I remember bouncing up and down on my father's shoulders as he walked down the winding staircase from our tiny second-floor apartment to the street below. Just outside our neighbor Ms. Wilkinson's apartment there was a parakeet living in a cage on the landing that we would pass each day on our way out of the building.

As I recounted these memories of my early childhood to my mother, she looked at me in disbelief. "You couldn't possibly remember those days," she said. "It was after your father had come home from the service and we'd moved to Providence, Rhode Island, where he was enrolled at Brown University. I'd take you down to the river to watch the university crew team practice in the fall. There's no way you could remember that time because you were only a year and a half old!"

Memory is a peculiar thing because, while we may consciously recall little snippets of life, such as those I shared, what we often *don't* consciously remember is the way those around us responded to what was happening in our lives at the time. Because we *were* present, however, we *do* remember, as those subconscious experiences become the blueprint for the way we deal with relationships and life.

Because they're unconscious memories, we may not even be able to see them when we act them out, even when they're as plain as day to other people. But just because we might not immediately recognize these beliefs doesn't mean that we'll never know what they are or how they impact our lives. We, along with the people around us, are playing them out every day in our lives. They're being mirrored back to us in the form of our most intimate romantic relationships, friendships, businesses, and careers—and even in the condition of our health. The world is nothing more and nothing less than a reflection of what we believe both as individuals and collectively, consciously and subconsciously.

The key here is that 90 percent or more of our daily actions are responses that come from the reservoir of information we accumulated during the first seven years of life. If our caretakers responded to the world in a healthy, life-affirming way, then we benefit from our memory of their reactions. Rarely, however, have I come across anyone who can honestly say that they were raised in such surroundings. The reality is that most of us learned our subconscious habits in an environment that was a mixed bag. Some of the beliefs that were so deeply instilled within us have led to positive and healing ways to deal with life's tests. Others have done just the opposite.

### Finding Your Subconscious Beliefs

Our positive beliefs seldom become a problem. We just don't hear people complaining about too much joy or being overcome by too many good things happening in their lives. It's the negative patterns that lead to the problems. Or perhaps more accurately, *it's our perception of those patterns as negative* that can become the root of life's greatest suffering. Almost universally, the experiences that cause people to feel stuck have roots in what are considered negative beliefs that we acquire early in life. And it's precisely because they're subconscious that it's often difficult for us to see them in ourselves.

For this very reason, I often invite seminar participants to complete a preprinted form asking them to identify characteristics of their childhood caretakers, especially the traits that they would consider negative. The purpose of the chart is to identify the subconscious impressions and beliefs that we formed of these characteristics *while we were children,* rather than the way we see them with the benefit of our adult experience today. (I touched on this briefly in *The Divine Matrix,* but here I'll actually invite you to do this exercise yourself.)

The process is quick, simple, and effective.

If you'd like to gain insight into subconscious beliefs that may be playing out in your life today, complete the information in Figures 9–11 on a separate piece of paper or in a journal, following the instructions noted in the captions.

*If we can recognize the patterns that surround us as the people, situations, and relationships of life, we'll have a good idea of the subconscious beliefs within us that are their source.*

| | Male | Female |
|---|---|---|
| **B**<br>**(+)** | | |
| **A**<br>**(–)** | | |

**Figure 9.** Instructions for filling out the chart to identify the positive and negative characteristics of your childhood caretakers:

- On the top section (B) list the positive (+) characteristics for both male and female caretakers. This can be anyone from birth and foster parents to older brothers, sisters, other relatives, or family friends. Regardless of who the people are, the question relates to those who cared for you in your formative years, until about the age of 15 or so.

- On the bottom section (A), list the negative (–) characteristics for the same caretakers. *Note:* Remember to base your list on the way you would have seen them with the innocence of a child.

- *Helpful hint:* Use single words, concise adjectives, or short phrases.

After finishing the preceding exercise in a seminar, participants randomly shout out the words or phrases that they've placed in their boxes. As I mentioned, the negative qualities are where we'll often find the clues to our most troubling unconscious patterns, so we begin with how we saw them in our male and female caretakers.

Immediately, something interesting begins to happen: As one person shares his or her memory, someone else is offering the same feeling—and often even the same word. A sampling of the terms from any program shows nearly identical words describing our primary caretakers:

| | | | |
|---|---|---|---|
| Distant | Controlling | Unavailable | Critical |
| Judging | Jealous | Strict | Mean |
| Cold | Fearful | Dishonest | Unfair |

There's a lightness that fills the room, and everyone begins to laugh at what they see. If we didn't know better, we'd think we all came from the same family. How can so many people from such diverse backgrounds have such similar experiences? The answer to this mystery is the pattern that runs deeply in the fabric of our subconscious beliefs.

After completing the chart in Figure 9 together, we answer the question in Figure 10. While there are myriad things that would have made our lives better, this is asking what we *really* wanted from our caretakers.

While I don't want to taint your response with my suggestions, examples sometimes help. Past identifiers have been things such as love, companionship, attention, and so forth.

| | What Did You Want and Need Most from Your Caretakers? |
|---|---|
| C | |

**Figure 10.** In single words or brief phrases, list the things that were most important for you to receive from your childhood caretakers. *This time when you answer the question, do so from the perspective of where you are in your life today, as an adult.* Once again, use single words or brief phrases.

The next part of our exercise is to fill out the chart in Figure 11. Its purpose is to identify any recurring frustrations that you recollect in your childhood. They can be as big or as small as you remember them, and can range from such things as not being heard or held, to wanting acknowledgment for your accomplishments.

As children, we're very creative and will usually find a way to get the things we need one way or another. Following each childhood frustration in the chart, describe how you dealt with it. How did you maneuver around the obstacles in your life to get what you needed? These can be simple themes—for example, "Broke the rules," "Withdrew from the world," or "Found another source of support."

| | 1. Your Frustrations | 2. How Did You Address Your Frustrations? |
|---|---|---|
| D | | |

**Figure 11.** In the chart above, describe your childhood frustrations and what you did to deal with them. As in the preceding steps, to the degree that you can, respond with single words or short phrases, as it will be easier to work with the answers.

The last part of this exercise in discovering your subconscious beliefs is to complete the simple form that follows, using the single words or short phrases drawn from the charts in Figures 9, 10, and 11. As you're doing so, please bear in mind that there are no absolutes. Rarely are patterns so clearly defined in life that you can say this is "absolutely so" or that this is "definitely" what has happened. What you're looking for here are themes and subconscious patterns that may be playing out in your life today.

To find out for yourself, complete the following statements on a separate piece of paper or in a journal.

**Statement 1:** I sometimes attract people into my life who are [finish this sentence with the words from Figure 9 (A)] _____.

**Statement 2:** I want them to be [finish with the words from Figure 9 (B)] _____ . . .

**Statement 3:** . . . so that I can have [finish with the words from Figure 10 (C)] _____.

**Statement 4:** I prevent myself from getting this sometimes by [finish with the words from Figure 11 (D2)] _____.

Don't be surprised if you begin to see patterns within your life history lighting up even before your chart is completed. In a moment I'll go over how these can lead you to understand your subconscious beliefs.

Once we start the momentum of identifying our patterns, it seems as if everything else just falls into place. A sample of what a completed chart might describe is the following:

**Statement 1:** I sometimes attract people into my life who are _angry, unavailable, judgmental._

**Statement 2:** I want them to be _loving, understanding, accepting_ . . .

**Statement 3:** . . . so that I can have _love, companionship._

**Statement 4:** I prevent myself from getting this sometimes by _withdrawing from the world, breaking the rules._

This simple exercise is a powerful tool to help you see patterns of your true beliefs, which are a by-product of memories, perceptions, judgments, and desires. By answering each question honestly, you're able to piece together the elements of your subconscious beliefs that may shed new light on the experiences that you've drawn into your life.

As I mentioned before, there are no absolutes when it comes to subconscious beliefs. This exercise is designed to provide a guideline and identify general patterns only. Here's what the information in the completed chart tells you:

— **Statement 1** helps you recognize that you sometimes now attract, or have in the past attracted, people into your life with the very characteristics that you *least* liked in your own childhood caretakers. While it may not be a conscious choice on your part to find such individuals, it's no coincidence either. Because you perceived these qualities as negative when you were a child and had a strong aversion to them then, you created an emotional "charge" on them. Your dislike for the negative quality (such as criticism or being ignored) becomes the magnet that draws it right into your life as an adult.

Of course, these characteristics often are overshadowed by other, preferred ones that you're also drawn to in a positive way. This is common in romantic relationships and friendships, where early on we tend to see only the favorable attributes that we want to see. An initial attraction of romance or trust lures us into a relationship that will ultimately ignite our deepest and strongest aversions.

This may be why it's not unusual in the heat of an argument to hear the comparison of our friend or partner to our mother, father, or another childhood caretaker. It honestly feels that way because our adult relationships are mirroring the full range of our caretakers' responses to the world. On a subconscious level, we may develop the belief that those with "bad" qualities are bad people.

— **Statement 2** helps you see that the things you often expect from others are the very qualities that you considered good or positive in your primary caretakers. So it's not surprising that the expressions of love, nurturing, caring, and thoughtfulness that you look for in your most intimate relationships are what you perceived as positive early in life. They were beneficial to you then, and you still see them that way as an adult. You believe that they're good and that those who possess these qualities are good people.

— **Statement 3** brings an awareness of the things that you want and need most in life from the perspective of a child. Ultimately, the answer to this question illustrates that while you may be grown up now, you're still searching for essentially the same things that you sought when you were young—only now you typically go about getting them in more sophisticated and adult ways.

— While Statements 1–3 are interesting and may shed some light on patterns in your life, **Statement 4** is the main reason for doing this exercise. It suggests that subconsciously you actually may be short-circuiting the great joy and accomplishments that are possible in your life by trying to get your needs met using updated versions of the techniques that you learned as a child.

We're creatures of habit. Once we find something that works, we tend to stick with it. This can be healthy if that "something" is an honoring and life-affirming process. But it can be *un*healthy and destroy our deepest dreams if it's dishonoring to us or to others and is a devious way to overcome life's obstacles to get what we want and need.

Just to reiterate, there are no certainties in this exercise. The questions are designed to illuminate possible patterns of subconscious beliefs that may be blocking us from joy, success, and abundance in our lives today. We can't see these patterns in ourselves, yet they're revealed in the exercise because they're mirrored in our relationships.

Whenever I offer this exercise in a seminar, I complete my own copy of the chart. And each time I do, I learn something new. While I've lost count of how many times I've shared the process, I always find myself thinking of a different characteristic that describes my caretakers or remember another way that I navigated childhood obstacles. The reason why our answers can vary is because we change throughout our lives. And as we do, our perspectives shift as well, including those on our past.

This chart offers a powerful window into the complex world of subconscious beliefs. Just because the exercise is quick and easy, however, please don't think that it isn't effective. I've personally witnessed the insights from these simple questions turn around extreme cases, ranging from people on the brink of taking their own lives, to health conditions that were stealing the life from someone who *wanted* to live. And all participants did was peek into the first few years of their memory and realize that their most troubling beliefs weren't even theirs, but came from their caretakers.

So I invite you to use this chart more than once, especially when you're going through major changes or challenges in your life. During those times, the issues that are sometimes the most difficult to see in yourself tend to surface in your relationships with others. When they do, it's generally in a way that can't be missed! It's also on those occasions that your deeply hidden beliefs are most available for healing through integration into your conscious awareness.

### Believing into Reality

It's not uncommon for people to have resistance to the idea that belief plays a huge unseen role in their lives. After all, how much power could something as simple as a belief really have?

We live in a world where we're conditioned to think that change happens as a result of brute force. When we want to see something done differently, we're taught that we must hammer the existing reality into submission for that change to happen. Whether it's the surgical removal of a tumor, shouting our vote into acceptance, or the military overthrow of a dictator, the conventional thinking has been that if it doesn't take a lot of effort, it probably isn't going to work. So is it really possible to change our world, our bodies, or anything at all through an invisible power that everyone else already has?

> **Belief Code 18:**
> In our greatest challenges of life we often find that our deeply hidden beliefs are exposed and available for healing.

These are good questions. Perhaps the best way to answer them is through an example. The following story illustrates the power that can come from the focus of one person's belief—in this case, that of one man to mirror through his body the suffering experienced by someone else. In this example, we find that not only was the person with the belief changed forever, but so were the lives of those who witnessed it.

❋

I arrived at the conference venue late in the afternoon to prepare for a presentation I'd be giving bright and early the next morning. After meeting some friends who'd come early for the same reason, we agreed that we would have a late lunch/early dinner and take the rest of the evening to work on our programs.

We'd been seated in the restaurant for only a couple of minutes when we noticed that something was happening at the entrance, where a number of guests were waiting to be seated. It was hard *not* to notice: The typical buzz of the 200 or so friends, presenters, and hotel guests who were having their meals had suddenly come to an abrupt halt. Like the hushed wave that moves through an audience when they realize that the show is about to begin, the whole restaurant quickly became silent. All eyes were gazing toward the front of the room at the group of people who'd just entered and the man whom they surrounded. I was one of those who were more than a little taken aback by what I saw.

As I watched the hostess guide the entourage of ten or so people between the tables, I couldn't look away from the man at the center of the group. He was taller than those around him. He had peaceful eyes; thick, dark, curly hair; and an equally thick and very full beard that covered most of his face. He was dressed in an ensemble of loose-fitting garments, all white, which were almost indistinguishable from one another—already in contrast to the Levi's and T-shirts that were the uniform for most of the people in the room. One thing was certain: This man was not a "local." But that wasn't what had drawn our attention.

Through the combination of his garments, hair, and beard, this man immediately drew a powerful response from the people in the room. I heard whispers comparing him to Jesus. As he walked past our table, his eyes met mine and we acknowledged one another with a slight nod of our heads. Then I saw clearly what I'd only suspected from a distance.

From the center of his forehead down to the bridge of his nose and across the space between his eyebrows, the wound couldn't be mistaken at such close range: It was a cross. But not just any cross. There, emblazoned upon the man's face, was an open wound that formed the perfect proportions of a Christian cross. With no bandages to cover it, it was defined by a combination of fresh and drying blood.

As he passed and raised his hand in a subtle gesture of hello, I could see that his forehead wasn't the only place where his body had an injury. His palms were wrapped in white gauze that matched his garments—that is, except where the blood had seeped through the bandages and stained it. While he walked toward his table, others following in his group simply glanced at me with a bit of an irritated look, as if to say, *What's the matter, haven't you ever seen a man bleed like this before?* They were obviously used to being on the receiving end of such stares as they made their public visits. Almost instantly one word popped into my mind, and, as quietly as I could, I whispered it under my breath almost instinctively: "*Stigmata!* This man is living with stigmata!"

As the group was seated, gradually the buzz resumed in the room as the other diners went back to their meals and conversation. While I'd certainly read of the phenomenon of stigmata—instances where people identify so strongly with Jesus's wounds from the crucifixion that they manifest them on their bodies as well—I'd never actually seen a living example. Yet here was precisely such a person, sitting about 30 feet away from me, preparing to have a meal in a hotel restaurant. I'd soon discover that he was scheduled at the last minute to be one of the presenters at the conference.

Immediately, my mind began to race with questions. The obvious one was simply: *How does it happen?* How could a man's beliefs be so powerful that they could manifest as the physical wounds that I was seeing on his body? I'd later discover that there were additional wounds on his feet and torso, all matching those of Christ following the crucifixion described in the Gospels.

What was it about an event that happened 2,000 years ago that could influence this man so powerfully today? Or, more precisely, what was it about this man's feelings regarding that event that had such an impact on his life? The answer to this question, and the mystery of the placebo effect, are both pointing researchers in a direction that has made the science of medicine a little less certain.

### Belief Over Body

For the last three centuries, we've trusted the language of science to explain the universe and how things work. There's nothing in our traditional scientific model that explains a stigmata. When scientists witness such a bizarre phenomenon, there's a tendency to chalk it up to an anomaly. It's simply a fluke that they're comfortable placing into a category named "unsolved mystery," to be reexamined at some other time. It could be that in doing so in the past, we've ignored the very things that show us how the world really works.

Could a person's belief be so powerful that it actually mirrors his or her deepest feelings in the flesh of his or her body? Absolutely! While research on the placebo effect may not be as compelling to look at as a Christian cross emblazoned across a man's forehead, this is precisely what those and similar studies are telling us. When we believe that something is true, our belief combines with other forces in the field of Planck's matrix to give instructions to the body that make it come true. Sometimes the effects are visible in the physical world beyond our bodies, as we saw in the peace experiment in the Middle East. Or, in the case of stigmata, they're mirrored within the body that's having the feelings.

Consciously or subconsciously, our beliefs are part of the information that surrounds our world and us. From the regeneration of organs and skin to the healings that were described in the placebo experiments, the stuff we're made of conforms to the template of our deepest beliefs. And this is where the new discoveries of cell biology become so exciting, because they're saying the same thing—and they're doing so in the language of science.

The recent acknowledgment that the field "out there" is influencing how the stuff we're made of works inside of our cells sent a shock wave through the world of the traditional life sciences. Biologists steeped in the belief that DNA is the key to unlocking the mysteries of life have had to reconsider their position in light of the studies showing that genes are responding to information from the field surrounding them. What's important is that our beliefs—the electrical and magnetic waves created by our hearts—are part of that field. In other words, while DNA is certainly important—and is definitely a code that carries the language of life in our cells—there's another force that's telling it what to do.

It's this huge reassessment that has led to an entire new branch of biology called *epigenetics,* defined as the study of "hidden influences upon the genes"—influences that can come from a number of sources, including the beliefs that control our DNA.[8] This line of thinking is writing us back into the equation of life as powerful agents of change. These are the insights that will lead us to understand things such as the placebo effect and will explain why a man's belief about something that happened 2,000 years ago can manifest as the wounds on his body today.

It's often said that what we hold to be true of our world may be more important than what really exists. The reason? If we believe something clearly enough, our subconscious will transform our belief into the reality that we believed to begin with! In other words, it appears that the adage is true: "We'll see it when we believe it."

As the popular motivational speaker Robert Collier recognized more than a century ago, "Our subconscious mind cannot tell the difference between reality and an imagined thought or image."[9] So for someone who powerfully identifies with the experience of Jesus's crucifixion, it shouldn't be so surprising to see his subconscious mind direct his body to create those precise wounds on him. In his belief, he is living Jesus's Passion as a reality.

�֍

Once we encounter something that tells us our previous way of seeing the world is incomplete, or even flat-out wrong, the hard part of changing our beliefs is behind us. Our direct experience is the catalyst that breaks the bonds of perception that may have kept us locked into our old way of seeing. Then we're on the path to something new, a different point of view. The key is that it happens spontaneously. We don't necessarily find ourselves sitting at a Starbucks and saying to ourselves, *Okay, now I need something new to believe in.* The new belief happens automatically in the presence of the experience that gives us a reason to embrace it.

The question now is less about whether or not belief influences our bodies and our lives, and more about the beliefs that form the foundation of the health or disease, abundance or lack, and joy or suffering of our experiences. In short, what is it that we believe?

This isn't a matter of what you *think,* or what you would *like* to *think,* you believe. Rather, this may be the single most powerful and revealing question that you may ever ask yourself: *What do you really believe?*

# What Do You Believe?: The Great Question at the Core of Your Life

*"Do not believe in anything simply because you have heard it.
Do not believe in anything simply because it is spoken and
rumored by many, or merely on the authority of your teachers
and elders. But after observation and analysis, when you find that
anything agrees with reason, then accept it and live up to it."*
— **Buddha** (c. 563 B.C.E.–c. 483 B.C.E.)

*"There are two ways to be fooled. One is to believe what
isn't true; the other is to refuse to believe what is true."*
— **Søren Kierkegaard** (1813–1855), philosopher

We've described how our beliefs work and why they have the power to change our bodies and our lives. With such a force shaping everything from the success of our relationships to how long we live, it makes tremendous sense to ask about our own beliefs. Where do they come from? How do they play out in life? And perhaps most important, <u>what</u> do we believe—not what do we *think* we believe or what would we *like* to believe, but what do we *truly* believe about our world, other people, and ourselves? The honest answer to these seemingly innocent questions opens the door to our greatest realizations—and our deepest healing. In the absence of such understanding, life's deepest mysteries often remain unsolved.

### Dying from a Belief

Early in life we develop our core beliefs—basic ideas that we accept about ourselves, other people, and our world. They can either be positive or negative, life affirming or life denying. Childhood experiences are often where our core beliefs begin. After repeatedly hearing that we don't deserve this or that early in life, for example, we may develop a core belief that we aren't worthy of receiving. Because such perceptions are often subconscious, it's not unusual to discover that they weave their way throughout our lives in unexpected ways. So an unconscious core belief that we aren't worthy of receiving may play out as a lifetime of lack that shows up in love, money, and success . . . and even life itself.

A few years ago a dear friend shared a story with me that brought tears to my eyes. It's a beautiful example of just how much power a core belief in our hearts can have over our lives. She described how her father had died at the age of 75 following a short battle with a particularly aggressive form of cancer. While she accepted my condolences when I told her that I was sorry for her loss, it was what I heard next that makes this story so relevant.

Although my friend and her family were certainly saddened by the loss of the man who was so central to their lives, she said that they weren't really surprised. Ever since she'd been a young girl, she'd heard her father affirm that he wouldn't live beyond 75 years of age. Although he was a healthy and vital man and had no real reason to expect that his life would end abruptly, it was just something that he believed. Since *his* own father had died at 75, in his mind that life span was the model that helped him structure his time on Earth.

He'd shared his belief with his family for as long as anyone could remember. Although he may have wanted to live longer, and he enjoyed spending time with his friends and family, he wasn't angry or disappointed at the thought of leaving the world after only seven and a half decades of life. Based on the previous chapters of this book and the power that we know is held in our beliefs, what comes next should be no surprise.

On the man's 75th birthday, his family and friends gathered around him to help him celebrate. Shortly thereafter, he was stricken with cancer. Following a brief battle with the disease, he died—just as he believed he would—before reaching the 76-year mark of life on Earth.

There are numerous case histories that suggest that the power of a belief can be "inherited" if it's accepted and held by others. The studies show that beliefs can even be passed on from one generation to the next. If they're positive and life affirming, the ability to perpetuate them for many generations is a good thing. If, on the other hand, they're limiting and life denying, they can cut short the one experience that we cherish so deeply yet often take for granted: that of life itself.

All it takes is one person, however, in any generation to heal the limiting beliefs. In doing so, such an individual will have healed them not only for him- or herself, but also for countless generations to come . . . just as the next example illustrates.

### Healing an "Inherited" Belief

When I heard about my friend's father, it reminded me of a similar situation that I'd seen more than 20 years earlier. This story has a different ending, however, and demonstrates the power of one individual to heal the belief in an early death that had lasted for at least two generations.

Even by today's standards, the late 1970s was a time of tremendous tension and uncertainty in the world. Americans were still reeling from the oil embargo that had brought the country to its knees just a few short years earlier. In late 1979, Iranian militants had taken more than 50 Americans hostage in a blatant act of aggression that left the world wondering how the U.S. would respond. And all of these things were happening during one of the most frightening conflicts (even though it was undeclared) in the history of the nation, the Cold War.

It was during this time that I'd just been hired by a large energy corporation to use their new state-of-the-art, high-speed, room-sized computers (miniaturization was still a few years away) to explore the ocean's floor for undiscovered "wrinkles" and faults—indications of possible new energy sources. For both the nation in general and the corporate culture in which I found myself immersed, the last thing on anyone's mind was the possibility that our beliefs could influence reality.

Within a few days of beginning my new job, I met a woman hired at about the same time. She would describe the situation of a life-and-death belief so powerful that she and her family accepted it as an "inherited" fact.

As new employees, we'd just completed the customary orientation process earlier in the day. The seemingly endless stream of presentations included a dizzying array of insurance policies and packages. Following the orientation, my new colleague and I found ourselves engaged in conversation about the policies with an intensity that surprised us both.

While I certainly agreed that it was a responsible thing for everyone to have the best insurance possible, after a full day of presentations, all of the packages began to look the same. I was ready to choose one and move on. I didn't understand why my friend was so concerned about even the smallest details of precisely how the benefits actually worked. My thinking was that the odds were in our favor that we wouldn't need them for years. I didn't understand why it was so important for her to know the intricacies of how to file a claim, how quickly she would receive a check in the event of her husband's death, and how soon the policy could go into effect—that is, until she shared the following story.

"None of the men on my husband's side of the family live beyond the age of 35," she told me in a matter-of-fact tone of voice.

"Really?" I answered, probably looking as baffled as I sounded.

"Oh yeah," she said, without even giving it a second thought. She'd obviously had this conversation before. "*There's nothing we can do, you know. It's all genetic.* My husband's grandfather died at the age of 35. His father died when *he* was 35. A couple of years ago, his brother died at 35. My husband is 33 now, and he's next, so we have to plan now," she explained.

I couldn't believe what I was hearing. While I didn't know my co-worker's husband, I learned that they'd known each other for a long time and had two beautiful children together. If she really expected that he'd follow the pattern of the men in his family, then her interest in the insurance suddenly made tremendous sense to me. She honestly felt that she'd be using it soon.

At the same time, a part of me just couldn't accept the whole story. It's not that I don't feel that the kinds of things my co-worker was describing can happen. It's just that I believe they don't *have to.* The idea of being the victim of a limited life span because it runs in the family didn't ring true for me. I couldn't help but think that maybe their story could have another ending; perhaps something would change in their lives and her husband would be the first one to break the cycle that had plagued his family for as long as anyone could remember. Now that she'd told me about the "curse" and we were to work together, the door was open for the deep, often-emotional conversations that were to follow.

I also learned quickly that something like a spouse's life span can be a really sensitive subject, and talking about it can be a little tricky—especially with someone you share an office with.

Although the research has shown an unmistakable correlation between our core beliefs and the health, vitality, and longevity of our bodies, it's also easy to misinterpret this kind of connection. It's all about the way that information is shared.

On the one hand, I believe that no one wakes up one morning and *consciously chooses* to manifest a physical condition that will bring pain into their life and suffering to their loved ones. On the other hand, I also know beyond any reasonable doubt that by changing a belief, we can renew the health and vitality of our bodies. The key is to find a way to share such miraculous possibilities without sounding judgmental or in any way suggesting that a life-threatening condition is someone's "fault."

And this is what I did my very best to offer my friend. Soon we found ourselves immersed in lunchtime conversations exploring the world as quantum possibilities and the power of belief to choose among them in life.

I can't tell you for sure how this story ended, because I left the company a few years later. It's been more than 20 years since I've spoken to my former office mate. What I *can* tell you with certainty, however, is this: By the time I did leave, my friend's husband had reached, *and passed,* his 35th birthday. At the time of my farewell lunch, he was in good health and definitely alive! To his family's surprise and relief, he'd broken what they saw as their family's multigenerational "genetic curse." Because he'd transcended the limits that others had held for him in their beliefs, he gave himself a reason to think of his life differently, as well as offering his family and friends grounds to do the same.

Sometimes that's all it takes: one person doing the seemingly impossible in the presence of others. In witnessing the limits broken, they can then hold the new possibility in their minds, because they've personally experienced it.

When we hear stories such as the preceding ones, we find ourselves asking, "Is it simply a coincidence?" Is it a fluke that someone's life span *just happens* to conform precisely to his or her expectation or those of his or her family members? Or is it something more?

With the renaissance of interest in the mind/body connection that began in the late 20th century, new studies are appearing almost weekly in scientific and mainstream journals that identify a direct link between the way we think and feel in our bodies and the way we function physically. It's that connection that plays out in our everyday lives, just as my two friends' loved ones demonstrate.

While their stories illustrate the power that a belief can hold for one person, could that power run even deeper in a way that affects us all? Is it possible that, collectively, we share in a belief that's so common, and affects us on such a deep level, that it has actually established the limits of the human life span? And if so, can it be healed, and the limit changed? The answer to both of these questions is *yes.* The source of such a belief may surprise you.

### Do We Die Before Our Time?

Have you ever wondered why we die after only 70 or 100 years?

Aside from the obvious trauma of such things as war, murder, accidents, and poor lifestyle choices, what is the real cause of death in humans? Why is it that the odds of continuing a healthy, vital, and meaningful life seem to work against us as we pass what's often considered "midlife" and later approach the 100-year mark?

Among scientists, medical professionals, and scholars alike, there's agreement that our bodies have a miraculous ability to sustain life. Of the estimated 50 trillion or so cells that reside within the average human, most are documented to have the ability to repair themselves and reproduce throughout our life span. In other words, we're constantly replacing and rebuilding ourselves from the inside out!

Until recently, scientists believed that there were two exceptions to the phenomenon of cell regeneration. Interestingly, these special cases are the cells of the two centers that are most closely identified with the spiritual qualities that make us who we are: our brain and our heart. *Although new studies have now shown that the cells of these organs do have the ability to regenerate themselves, it also appears that they're so resilient that they can last a lifetime and don't necessarily need to!*

So, we're back to the original question: *Why does the upper limit of our life span appear to hover around the 100-year mark?* What it is that takes our lives?

With the exception of misused medicines and misdiagnosed conditions, the greatest killer of adults over the age of 65 is heart disease. I find this statistic fascinating because of the work that our hearts are built to do and how well they do it. The average human heart beats approximately 100,000 times daily—equaling more than 35 million times a year—and pumps six quarts of blood through approximately 12,000 miles of arteries, vessels, and capillaries every 24 hours. Our hearts appear to be so vital to who and what we are that they are the first organs to form in our mothers' wombs, even before our brains.

In engineering terms, when the success of an entire project depends upon a single piece of equipment, that component is given the status of "mission critical." In the space program, for example, when a rover will be landing on Mars and there will be no one around to fix something that might break, the engineers must do one of two things to assure the success of the mission. They either: (1) construct the one piece of the rover that the whole mission depends upon—*the mission-critical piece*—with such precision that it can't go wrong, or (2) build backup systems, and backups to the backups. Sometimes they even do both.

Clearly, the miraculous organ that feeds lifeblood to every cell inside us has developed—either by conscious design or natural processes—to be the body's most self-healing and longest-lasting mission-critical piece of "equipment." So anytime the loss of someone we love is attributed to the "failure" of such a magnificent organ, we've got to ask ourselves *what really* happened to that person. Why would the first organ to develop in someone's body—and one that performs *so* impressively, and for *so* long, with cells that are *so* enduring that they don't even need to reproduce—simply stop working after only a few short decades? It makes no sense . . . unless there's another factor that we haven't considered.

Modern medicine typically attributes heart conditions to an array of physical and lifestyle factors, ranging from cholesterol and diet to environmental toxins and stress. While these determinants may be accurate on a purely chemical level, they do little to address the actual reason why the conditions exist. What does "failure of the heart" really mean?

Perhaps it's not a coincidence that all the lifestyle factors linked to heart failure are also linked to the force that speaks to the universe itself: human emotion. Is there something that we *feel* over the course of our lives that can lead to the catastrophic failure of the most important organ in the body? The answer is *yes.*

### The Hurt That Kills

A growing body of evidence from leading-edge researchers suggests that *hurt* can cause the failure of our hearts. Specifically, the unresolved negative feelings that underlie chronic hurt—*our beliefs*—have the power to create the physical conditions that we recognize as cardiovascular disease: tension, inflammation, high blood pressure, and clogged arteries.

This mind/body relationship was documented recently in a landmark study at Duke University directed by James Blumenthal.[1] He identified long-term experiences of fear, frustration, anxiety, and disappointment as examples of the kind of heightened negative emotions that are destructive to the heart and put us at risk. Each is part of a broader umbrella that we commonly identify as "hurt."

Additional studies support the existence of this relationship. Therapist Tim Laurence, codirector of the Hoffman Institute in England, describes the potential impact of our failure to heal and forgive old hurts and disappointments. "At the very least," he says, "it cuts you off from good health."[2] He supports this statement by citing a number of studies that show, as did Blumenthal's, that physical conditions of anger and tension can lead to problems that include high blood pressure; headaches; lowered immunity; stomach problems; and, finally, heart attacks.

What Blumenthal's study showed was that teaching people to "tone down" their emotional responses to life situations could prevent heart attacks. This is precisely the point of healing our hurt—specifically, what we believe to be true about the things that have hurt us.

Clearly, this study, along with others, isn't suggesting that it's bad or unhealthy to feel negative emotions in the short term. When we do encounter these feelings in life, they are indicators—personal gauges—telling us that we've had an experience that's asking for attention and healing. It's only when we ignore them, and the beliefs that underlie them, and they go on for months, years, or a lifetime without being resolved that they may become a problem.

Could the answer to our question of why we die be that

> **Belief Code 19:**
> Our beliefs about unresolved hurt can create physical effects with the power to damage or even kill us.

through the pain of life's disappointments we've hurt ourselves to death? Blumenthal's studies suggest, "Perhaps when people talk about dying of a broken heart, they are really saying that intense emotional reactions to loss and disappointment can cause a fatal heart attack."[3] In the language of their time, ancient traditions hint at precisely this possibility.

### The First 100 Years Are the Toughest

So why does the maximum human age seem to hover around the 100-year mark? Why not 200 years, 500, or even longer? If we're to believe accounts in the Old Testament (or the Torah in the Jewish tradition), many ancient people measured their lives in terms of centuries rather than the decades that we use today. The book of Genesis, for example, states that Noah lived for 350 years *after* the Great Flood. If he were 950 years old when he died, as the text also says, this would mean that he was fit and vital enough to build the ark that would ensure the survival of the entire human race when he was 600 years old!

According to the Scriptures, those who lived to advanced ages weren't simply shriveled husks of their former selves, meagerly hanging on to the frail thread of life. They were active and vital, enjoying their families, and even starting new ones. And why shouldn't they be? We clearly live in bodies that are built to last for a long time. And apparently they've done so in the past. So why not now? What's changed?

This is one of those places where we must cross the traditional boundary between science and spirituality for answers. Clearly there's more to us than the elements that make up the DNA of our bodies. Although science has yet to capture or digitally prove the soul's existence, we know that it's the mysterious force that animates the elements of our physical self. It's what brings the body to life. And this is where we find the heart of our answer. When our soul hurts, our pain is transmitted into the body as the spiritual quality of the life force that we feed into each cell.

The hundred years or so that we see as the duration of human life appears to be the limit of how long we can endure unresolved hurt in the soul. In other words, the century mark may be telling us how long we can bear the sadness and disappointments of life before they catch up with us. We can all attest to the pain that comes from watching the people we love, the pets we cherish, and experiences we grow attached to disappear from our lives. Could a lifetime of loss, disappointment, and betrayal have the power to disable even our strongest and most durable organ—the heart?

> **Belief Code 20:**
> When our soul hurts, our pain is transmitted into the body as the spiritual quality of the life force that we feed into each cell.

Absolutely! And there may be even more: The hurt that kills us could be even more ancient and go even deeper than we've imagined.

In addition to such obvious sources of pain, perhaps there's another one that's less apparent yet so big and universally shared that it's hard for us to bear even thinking about it. Across cultures and societies, creation stories state that to become individuals in this world, we must "break away" from a greater collective soul family. At the same time, one of the deepest universal fears is just that: being separate and alone.

Perhaps the great hurt that underlies all others is the pain of separation from a greater existence. If this is true, then maybe we miss our larger soul family so much that we try to fill the void by re-creating a sense of unity through smaller families here on Earth. It's no wonder, then, that their loss can be so devastating to us. It throws us right back into the pain of the original hurt.

For many people, it's their yearning to "hold on" to their families, their relationships, and memories of their past experiences that create the conditions that lead to their greatest suffering. They long for the pets they can never have again and the people they miss, and alcohol and drugs too often become the socially acceptable anesthetic used to numb such deep soul pain.

If we can find a way to appreciate the moments we share with those we love, as well as feel good about our time together when it ends, then we will have taken a giant step toward our greatest healing. From this perspective, the same principles that allow us to hurt ourselves into death also work in reverse—that is, they offer us the healing power of life. This key appears to be related to the way we feel about what life shows us.

While all of these are possibilities to think about, what we know for certain is this: There is a biological potential for our bodies to last much longer than they do and for us to live healthier and richer lives than many of us seem to experience at present. In addition to the physical elements, there is something that seems to be missing from the modern equation for longevity. Regardless of what we choose to call it, that "something" is a spiritual force that feeds and nourishes us. In the language of another time, the ancients left us instructions to make room for this vital force upon which all life depends. To lead long, healthy, and fulfilling lives, we must heal the limiting beliefs that lie at the core of our deepest hurts.

> **Belief Code 21:**
> The same principles that allow us to hurt ourselves into death also work in reverse, allowing us to heal ourselves into life.

Now that you know how unconscious beliefs can play out, it makes sense to take a look at the relationships of everyday life to reveal your own deeply held beliefs. Let's begin with love. What follows will help you to be very clear about where you are in relationship to this vital force in your life.

The three questions I'm about to pose to you may appear so simple at first that you might wonder why I would even ask them. And while they *are* obvious, in our busy lives we sometimes overlook the obvious in our effort to find fast answers and quick solutions. Sometimes it helps to just take a moment, sit back, and—with the greatest honesty and respect for ourselves—revisit the basics. Once we do, we can use our answers to direct us to our next step.

Rather than the collective "us" that we've been talking about so far, this is where the spontaneous healing of belief becomes individual. These questions are designed for you, so I will direct them to you in a personal way and ask them as if I were speaking with you. I invite you to answer the following:

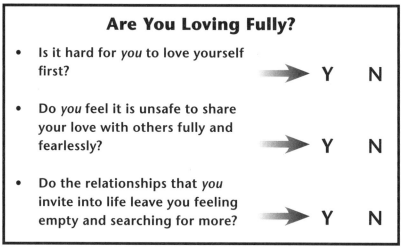

**Are You Loving Fully?**

- Is it hard for *you* to love yourself first? ➤ Y  N

- Do *you* feel it is unsafe to share your love with others fully and fearlessly? ➤ Y  N

- Do the relationships that *you* invite into life leave you feeling empty and searching for more? ➤ Y  N

**Figure 12.** Three simple questions designed to awaken the possibility of greater acceptance, longevity, and healing in your life. The way you answer them helps to identify anything that stands between you and your fullest experience of life-affirming love.

If your answer to any of the preceding questions is "yes," then what do you think the chances are that the hurt, disappointment, suffering, and betrayal that you've experienced in life stem from an unconscious belief that spills over into your conscious experiences? To find out, you'll need to look just a little deeper into a subtle belief that may explain why that "yes" is there. To do so, you'll have to answer one more simple yet revealing question, the Great Question that you—and only you—can answer for yourself.

### The Great Question at the Core of Your Life

There's a central belief that guides our lives, and it does so in ways that we may not even be aware of or think about. The reason why this belief can have so much power without our even knowing it exists is that it's unconscious. That's right—running on automatic pilot as an instinctive program in the back of our minds at this very moment is a core belief that's so powerful that it has been the template against which all others of our lives have been compared.

As diverse as your life has been, and as varied as all of your experiences appear, there's nothing that's happened that wasn't shaped through the eyes of this single belief. Without exception, all of your love and each of your fears; all of the chances in life that you've had the confidence to take and all of the ones that you were afraid to because you might fail; the health, vitality, and youth of your body; the way you age; and the success or failure of every relationship that you'll ever have with another person, yourself, your world, and the entire universe . . . all of these things, and more, boil down to what you claim in a single belief.

You can discover what that belief is for yourself by answering a single question—the Great Question—below. The way that you do so reveals the truth of a powerful subconscious belief that lies at the heart of your existence. The question is this:

*Do you believe that there is one source for everything that happens in the world, or do you believe that there are two opposite and opposing forces—good and evil—one that "likes" you and one that doesn't?*

That's it! It's brief. But please don't be deceived by the simplicity of these few words. They're also powerful, and profound. This is the one question that we must each answer at some point in our lives. And it is, perhaps, about the biggest relationship that we'll ever be asked to come to terms with. In its simplicity lies its elegance.

How you respond to the Great Question will prompt you to redefine the essence of who you believe you are and the way you feel about your life in the world. As you experience the clarity that the answer to this question provides, you're prompting your "inner pro-grammer" to shift and adjust the patterns that affirm life in your body. It all begins with this simple question. Here's how it works.

### The Template of Your Life

Your answer to the Great Question is the template of your life. If you believe that there are two separate forces that exist in the world, with two very different modes of expression, then you will always see the things that happen in life through the eyes of those polari-ties and that separation. Even though this may be an uncon-scious belief that you never talk about with others, and perhaps never even acknowledge to your-self, it can still dominate your acceptance of love and success in every relationship, each career, all your finances, and the quality of your health.

> **Belief Code 22:**
> Our belief in one force for everything that happens in the world, or two opposite and opposing forces—good and evil—plays out in our experience of life, health, relationships, and abundance.

This single, sometimes unconscious, belief can hijack the most powerful experiences of our lives, and do so without our even know-ing that it's happened.

For example, if we view the force of "light" as a friend who loves us and wants only the best for us, while believing that "darkness" doesn't care about us and wants to entice us into self-destructive patterns, then the world begins to look like the battleground between these forces. And when the world becomes the *battleground,* life becomes the *battle.* If we are convinced that the two forces are at odds with one another, we begin to see that conflict playing out in every belief, from how worthy we are of receiving love (see the chart in the previ-ous chapter) and success, to how deserving we are of life itself! In the presence of such a deeply held belief expressing itself with the power and reactive speed of our subconscious mind, it's not surprising, then, to find this battle manifesting as the chemistry of our bodies.

As we noted previously, for each *nonphysical* feeling, emotion, and belief that we create within our bodies, there is the *physical equivalent* of that experience that becomes the makeup of our cells. So we literally have what we may call "love chemistry" and "hate chemistry." With this fact in mind, what do you suppose happens when we live our lives believing that there are two basic forces in this world—one that is good and one that is bad, one that likes us and one that doesn't, one that is here to help us and one that is out to get us? The answer becomes obvious.

If we believe at the core of our being that life is a rare and precious gift to be nurtured, explored, and cherished, then the world looks like a beautiful place to do our exploring. It's rich in diverse cultures, experiences, and opportunities. The key here is that we must *believe* that we're safe before we can immerse ourselves in the benefits of such an experience. This is more than simply hoping or wishing it were true. We must accept and believe it to the core of our being.

So you're saying "Yeah, right! Tell me again, just where is it that this safe world exists?" and I would agree that if we look to the mass media and popular opinion, we have every reason to believe that our world is anything *but* safe.

On the other hand, if we truly believe at the very core of our being that this is a dangerous world, and we embody that belief each day in our lives, we'll see it play out in everything from our jobs and careers to our relationships and health. Even when new opportunities come our way, we'll feel that we aren't supported, ready, or worthy of accepting them. We'll be afraid to take risks, we'll feel unworthy of having the job or the romance that brings us true joy, and we'll find ourselves settling for whatever comes our way.

If we have no reason to believe differently, it's not surprising that we may find the battle that we subconsciously believe in playing out in the cells of our bodies—they will interpret our beliefs as the instructions to produce the chemistry that steals from us the very experience that we cherish the most: life itself!

Sometimes this outpicturing of beliefs in our bodies is subtle. It's a blessing when it is, because it gives us the opportunity to recognize the signals of our fear and address them before it's too late. Sometimes, however, it's not so subtle.

### Our Body: The Mirrored Answer to the Great Question

My grandfather was a man of habit. When he found something that worked for him, he stayed with it. That may explain how he and my grandmother remained married for more than 50 years. After she died, and he was living with his brother, my relationship with him changed. We developed an easy friendship and deeper level of sharing that lasted for the rest of his life.

Grandpa's favorite place to eat was at the local franchise of the fast-food chain Wendy's. When I would visit from my out-of-state job on holidays or special occasions, I'd always set a full day aside to take Grandpa anywhere he wanted to go. It was *our* day together, and I'd ask him again and again, "Grandpa, where would you like to spend the day?" I always followed up my question with a list of beautiful restaurants and cafés, all of which were close to his home in the city. While he would listen carefully, and actually mulled over each option in his mind, his answer would always be the same, and I knew what it would be: "Wendy's."

A trip to Wendy's was an all-day affair. We'd generally arrive in the late morning, just before the lunchtime rush of businesspeople who had to be in and out in an hour. We'd sit and watch them come and go until we were the only two left. Then I'd listen to his stories of what our country was like during the Great Depression, or we'd talk about the problems of the day and what they meant for the future of the world. As evening came and the dinner crowd made the restaurant too noisy to talk, he'd finish the cheeseburger and bowl of chili that he'd nursed for hours, and I'd take him home.

One day when Grandpa was sitting across from me at our favorite table, he suddenly leaned toward me and just slumped over onto the table. He was fully awake and conscious. His eyes were clear, he could speak perfectly, and for all intents and purposes, everything else seemed fine. He just couldn't sit upright in his chair. It was on that day at Wendy's that we discovered Grandpa had developed a disease in his 80s that's often found in women in their 30s.

Called *myasthenia gravis,* this condition makes itself known when a person's body becomes unresponsive to the intention to move muscles, stand up straight, or even do something as simple as hold his or her head up. Medically, it's defined as an autoimmune disorder that results when the substance that normally carries the instructions between a person's nerves and muscles (acetylcholine) is absorbed by a special chemical—one produced by the person's own body.

So while my grandfather could think a thought that commanded his body to "sit upright," for example, and his brain would *send* the signal of that thought to his body, the muscles would never receive it. The chemical would "hijack" the signal. In other words, my grandfather had developed a condition where his body worked against itself in a battleground between two conflicting kinds of chemistry—one that produced everything he needed to function normally, and the other preventing those functions from ever happening. Between my travels, I spent as much time as I could with my grandfather and tried to help him deal with his experience while I learned about his condition.

During our time together, I found out something very interesting about his life and the history of our country—something that I believe was directly related to his condition. Grandpa was a young man working in a grocery store during the Great Depression. If you've ever talked to people who lived through that time, you're probably aware of the tremendous mark that the experience left on their lives. Seemingly overnight, everything changed: The economy ground to a halt, factories stopped their operations, stores closed, food became scarce, and people couldn't provide for their families. My grandfather was one of those people.

While he'd done everything that was humanly possible to bring food home for his new wife and the extended family who lived with them, and had done so relatively well, *in his mind* he believed that he'd failed. *And in his heart he felt guilty for his failure.* He felt ashamed that he'd been unsuccessful as a husband, son, son-in-law, and friend.

Before he died, I remember asking my grandfather about the Depression and his experience. And I recall the sadness that filled his face as he broke down and cried telling me the story. It was still so fresh in his mind, so present in his heart, and so much a part of his life, even after more than 60 years.

In my mind, the connection was obvious. My grandfather wasn't describing a passing sense of inadequacy about his life at an earlier time; rather, he was describing a tremendous sense of chronic and unresolved guilt that he felt in the present. He'd harbored it all of those years, and it had eventually become somatized as his physical experience. The connection was apparent because belief is a code, and our feelings of belief are its commands.

The chronic sense of helplessness that my grandfather had worked so hard to suppress—his subconscious belief that he was helpless— became the literal expression of his body. Through his mind/body relationship, his physical self recognized his beliefs as an unconscious command and masterfully produced the chemistry to match them. *Quite literally, his body became the helplessness of his belief.* I didn't have to search far to discover why the condition seemed to make its appearance so suddenly and at such a late stage in his life.

Not long before its onset, my grandfather's wife, my grand-mother, had been hospitalized for a cancerous condition that quickly took her life. Admitted to the hospital himself during her illness, my grandfather once again felt that he was helpless to do anything for the woman whom he'd loved for more than 50 years. To me, the correla-tion between the circumstances of my grandmother's death and the sudden occurrence of my grandfather's condition was too great to be a coincidence. It was the trigger that brought all of the old memories of inadequacy from the Great Depression right into the present.

Unfortunately, the mind/body connection hadn't been part of the training received by the medical staff caring for him at the time. To them, his was purely a physical condition, albeit a rare one for a man of his age, and they treated it as such. Each day for the rest of his life, my grandfather took 14 different medications to offset the symptoms and unwanted side effects that appeared to be linked to his belief that he was helpless to aid those he loved. While I know that this would never be the official medical diagnosis, the correlations are too compelling and the studies too convincing to suggest that his condition just "happened."

The power of our beliefs can work in either direction to become life affirming or life denying. Just as quickly as our unconscious beliefs can create the conditions that we found in the previous story of my colleague's husband, they can reverse those that threaten life itself. What makes this possibility so appealing is that our beliefs can be changed intentionally, in a moment in time. The key is to feel as if they're real rather than to simply think, hope, or wish that they would become true in our lives. In this way, *our* personal beliefs can overcome the conscious ones held by those we trust, such as doctors and friends. Sometimes all we need is for someone else to remind us that it's possible.

Ultimately, the key to transforming our most limiting beliefs may be found in healing our most intimate relationship in this world: the one that we identify between ourselves and the fundamental forces that make our world as it is—"light" and "darkness." It's our deepest, often-unconscious beliefs about these forces that form the basis for all other beliefs as they play out in life-affirming or life-denying ways.

### The Forces of Light and Darkness: Eternal Enemies or Misunderstood Realities?

Without a doubt, we do live in a world of opposites. And unquestionably, it's the tension between them that makes our reality what it is. From the charges of atomic particles to the conception of new life, it's all about pluses and minuses, "on" and "off," male and female. In theology, these opposites take on names and appearances that translate into the forces of light and dark, good and evil. While I'm not denying their existence, I *am* describing how it's possible to change what they mean in our lives and, by doing so, to redefine our relationship with them.

If we see life as a constant battle between light and dark, then we must judge everything in it through the eyes of opposites—and the world looks like a really scary place. Such a view requires that we identify with one or the other, and that we see it as better or more powerful. This is where we sometimes get into trouble with our own subconscious beliefs, as well as those of others. I remember thinking about this as a child—a lot.

Growing up in a conservative town in northern Missouri, I questioned what I'd been taught in school, in church, and in my family about the ideas of light and darkness, good and evil, and what these forces meant in my life. Something just didn't make sense to me. My conditioning led me to believe that we live in a world of good and evil, with both struggling to become the dominant force in my life. Those who meant well taught me that I could recognize the difference between the two by the way I experienced them: The things that hurt me were from the darkness, and the joy of feeling good was from the light. Implied in the idea of evil was the fear that something was out there—something horrible that was lurking, waiting for just the right time and just the right moment when, in an instant of weakness, all of the good that I'd ever achieved could be taken from me. If that were true, it meant this "something" was so awesome in its existence that it had power over us, power over *me.*

I struggled with the idea that we may actually be living in this kind of world—not so much because I didn't like it, but because it just didn't make sense. I knew that I'd have to reconcile what I'd been taught about the forces of light and dark with what they meant to *me* at some point in my life. Rather than a grand revelation in a single pivotal moment, however, that point came gradually as the result of a recurring dream that I had many times while I was in my 30s and 40s.

Perhaps not coincidentally, it came during some of the greatest challenges, and deepest hurts, of my life. I've always been a very visual person, so the graphic nature of this particular dream, coupled with the powerful emotions of what it means to me, comes as no surprise.

The dream always began in the same way: I saw myself alone in a place that was completely dark and totally empty. At first, there was nothing else around me, only the blackness that stretched everywhere and seemed endless. Gradually, however, something always came into view, something far, far away, off in the distance.

As my eyes adjusted to what I was seeing and I was able to move closer, I began to recognize faces. What I was seeing were people—a lot of them—some whom I knew and some I'd never seen before. (Interestingly, there were times I would find myself waiting at a stoplight in small-town traffic or walking through a busy airport, when I'd catch sight of someone I'd just seen only hours before in the dream.)

As the dream came into focus, I realized that in that mass of people was everyone I'd ever known or ever would know throughout my entire life, including all of my friends, all of my family members, and every person I've ever loved. And they were all there together, separated from me by a great divide that had opened in the blackness between us.

This is where the dream got really interesting. On one side of the divide was an abyss that was blindingly light, and on the other was an abyss that was the darkest of dark. Each time I tried crossing the divide to get to the people I love, I found myself pulled off balance by one side or the other. Every time I resisted falling into either the darkness or the light, I found myself back at the place where I began, missing everyone tremendously, as the people drew further and further away.

One night I had the dream and something changed. It began the same, so by the time I realized what was happening, I knew what to expect. On this particular night, I did something different: As I started to cross the divide and felt the darkness and the light pulling me in opposite directions, I didn't resist—and I didn't surrender. Instead, I changed the way I felt in their presence, and I altered what I believed about them.

Rather than judging one as "good" and one as "bad," or either as better or worse than the other, I allowed for both the light and the darkness to be present and let them become my friends. The instant that I did, something absolutely amazing happened: Suddenly, they looked different to me. In that difference they merged together, filled the divide, and became the bridge that led me to everyone I loved.

And once that happened, it was the end of the recurring dreams. While I've had others that taught me similarly, I've never had that particular one, in that way, again.

### The Cascade Effect of Healing

For several months before the healing in my recurring dream, I found myself in some of the most difficult relationships of my adult life. From friendships and business partnerships to family and even romantic partners, all seemed to be hopelessly spiraling out of control for reasons I simply didn't understand. As I'd come to discover through a recognition of the ancient Essene mirrors of relationship that I wrote about in *The Divine Matrix,* I'd developed a strong sense of what "should" and "shouldn't" be regarding honesty, integrity, and trust in others. And it was precisely my judgment of these qualities that proved to be the powerful magnet that kept pulling these relationships to me.

Almost immediately after the dream, something unexpected began to happen: Within a matter of only days, each of the people mirroring my judgments began to fall away from my life. I was no longer angry with them. I no longer resented them. I began to feel an odd sense of "nothingness" with regard to all of them. There was no intentional effort on my part to drive them away. Having redefined my relationship between light and dark, and recognizing my experiences with these people for what they were and not what my judgments made them out to be, I found that there was simply nothing left to keep them in my life. Each one began to fade from my day-to-day activities. Suddenly there were fewer phone calls from them, fewer letters, and fewer thoughts about them throughout the course of my day. My judgments had been the magnet that had held those relationships in place.

While this new development was interesting, within a few days something even more intriguing and even a little curious began to occur: I realized that other people who had been in my life for a long time, and with whom I wasn't in a conflict or a struggle of any kind, also began to fade away. Once again, there was no conscious effort on my part to end these relationships. They just didn't seem to make sense anymore. On the rare occasion when I did have a conversation with one of these individuals, it felt strained and artificial. Where there had been a common ground before, now there was uneasiness. Almost as soon as I noticed the shift in these relationships, I became aware of what for me was a new phenomenon.

Each of the relationships falling out my life had been based in the same pattern—the very one that had originally brought the people *into* my life. That pattern was the judgment of their actions viewed through my beliefs about light and darkness. In addition to being the magnet that drew the relationships to me, my judgment had also been the glue that had held them together. In its absence, the glue dissolved. I noticed what appeared to be a cascading effect that worked in this way: Once the pattern was recognized in one place, one relationship, its echo reverberated on many other levels of my life.

I suspect that this cascade effect of healing plays out often in our lives, although we may not always recognize it. In the preceding story, it happened so quickly that it would have been hard for me to miss it.

So I invite you to examine the relationships of your life, particularly the ones that have been difficult. When they suddenly seem to fade away for no apparent reason, their disappearance may be the indication that something in your beliefs has changed. It may just be that the glue of a perception has been healed and there's nothing left to keep those relationships close.

### Rewriting the Rules of the Ancient Battle

While the effects of our beliefs play out in our relationships and health, ultimately, we're talking about what we've viewed historically as the ancient battle mentioned earlier—the struggle between light and dark forces—manifesting in our bodies and in the world. For millennia, we've been conditioned to polarize these forces in our lives—to choose one and destroy the other. Although the battle is at least 2,000 years old, it's clearly with us today. We see it playing out through the technology and beliefs of the 21st century.

As with any conflict, we've got to ask ourselves, *If we're using the right strategy, then why hasn't somebody claimed victory?* Is it possible that the ancient struggle between light and dark isn't a battle to be won or lost in the usual sense of those words? What if the whole idea is to change the rules that keep it going? What if the secret to this battle is less about winning and more about how we change the core beliefs that hold it in place? Maybe the key to the great battle between light and dark plays out as little skirmishes right in front of us all of the time. If so, what can we learn from them?

I've known people, for example, who say that they only associate with others who are "of the light," or that the "forces of darkness" have taken over their friends and families. When they say that, I respond with a single question: I invite them to draw the line between the two—I ask them to show me where the light ends and the darkness begins. The moment they even attempt to do so, I can show them something even more powerful than the forces of light and dark themselves . . . because in the instant they begin to make that distinction, they've just fallen into the ancient trap that keeps them locked into the very polarizing beliefs that they tell me they're trying to escape!

Here's why: It's their judgment about good and evil—that one is better or more deserving of its existence than the other—that assures that they'll remain in the very condition that they've told me they want to change. I'm not suggesting that my friends condone or agree to what darkness can bring into our lives. There's a huge difference, however, between *judging* these forces and *discerning* that they exist and what they represent. And it's in this subtle yet significant distinction that we find the secret that allows us to rise above the polarity and heal the conflict between darkness and light—not just to survive it, *but to become greater* than the opposites that the battle itself allows. This is what I believe the dream that I described earlier was all about.

For some people, the thought of blending light and dark into a single potent force in our lives is something that they always believed possible yet maybe never quite knew how to realize. For others, the very thought of reconciling these two forces is the strangest thing they can imagine. It flies in the face of everything that they've ever been taught—and may even sound like heresy! It might, that is, until we look at the facts:

- **Fact 1:** The beliefs and feelings that we hold in our hearts are having an ongoing conversation with our brains in each moment of every day.

- **Fact 2:** During that dialogue, our hearts tell our brains to send "love chemistry" or "fear chemistry" into our bodies.

- **Fact 3:** Chronic love chemistry affirms and perpetuates life in our bodies.

- **Fact 4:** Chronic fear chemistry denies life in our bodies.

- **Fact 5:** To internalize the belief that two forces with different agendas are battling is to invite the combat into our bodies and our lives.

*Question:* Based on these facts, does it makes sense to remain engaged in an ongoing battle between light and dark by seeing one as a friend and the other as an enemy? Or does it make *more* sense to recognize that both are necessary, and in fact *are required,* for our three-dimensional world of electrons and protons, day and night, male and female, and life and death to exist?

While for some people describing our relationship with polarity as a battle is a metaphor, for others it plays out as the reality of their lives each day. Either way, what's key here is that the battle—actual or metaphorical—can only exist as long as our beliefs hold it in place.

As I healed my judgments with respect to light and darkness, that healing was reflected in every relationship: from romance and partnerships to business and finances. It was immediate, and it all began with a simple shift in what I held to be true about a belief that runs so deep in our collective subconscious that we may not even recognize it, yet is so universal that it affects all of us in each moment of every day. And it comes down to the Great Question of whether we believe that there are two separate forces (one that likes us and one that doesn't), or there is a single force that works in many and varied ways to give us our experience.

> **Belief Code 23:**
> To heal the ancient battle between darkness and light, we may find that it's less about defeating one or the other, and more about choosing our relationship to both.

Once we reconcile the powers of light and darkness as elements of the same force, the question becomes: *How do we use this unified force in our lives?* And this is where thinking of belief as a computer program becomes so potent. As it is with any program, if we know the code, we choose our limits. Understanding the language of belief gives us the power to choose the limits in our lives.

CHAPTER FIVE

# If You Know the Code,
# You Choose the Rules:
# Shattering the Paradigm
# of False Limits

. . . . . . . . . . . . . . . . . . . . . . . . . . . . . . . . . . . . . . . . . . .

*"[In a simulated reality] the simulators determine the laws,*
*and can change the laws, that govern their worlds."*
— **John D. Barrow,** astrophysicist and 2006 Templeton Prize winner

*"[Each person is born with an] infinite power, against*
*which no earthly force is of the slightest significance."*
— **Neville Goddard** (1905–1972), philosopher

. . . . . . . . . . . . . . . . . . . . . . . . . . . . . . . . . . . . . . . . . . .

Whether we actually believe that we're part of a cosmic simulation or simply use the idea as a metaphor for our relationship with our everyday world may be less important than the possibilities that such a notion implies. Metaphor or fact, the concepts give us a language with which to share the conversation, and a place to begin.

Either way, the experience of our lives is based on a program— a reality code—that translates possibilities into reality. Belief is that code. If we know how to create the right *kind* of belief, then our ideas of what "is" and "isn't" change forever. In other words, nothing is impossible in a world based in belief.

*Believing in Belief*

Years ago I remember seeing a late-night episode of a science-fiction program that aired every week on the black-and-white TV of the 1960s. Maybe you remember it as well: The show opened with the view of an allied warplane flying somewhere over Europe during World War II. Underneath it was a clear canopy that served as the observation seat for one of the airmen on the mission. It looked like a glass bubble that hung down from the fuselage and allowed the man inside to see all around him. From his vantage point, he could report enemy aircraft that the pilot and navigator couldn't see.

The general plot of the program is predictable. It comes as no surprise that the plane is attacked and heavily damaged by enemy antiaircraft fire. What happens next, however, isn't so predictable—and is the reason why I share this story.

Although the plane is damaged, it's still able to fly. The pilot decides to attempt an emergency landing at the nearest friendly airport. When he checks with the rest of his crew, though, he discovers that they've lost their landing gear in the attack. Suddenly, the pilot finds himself in a good news–bad news situation: The good news is that it looks like he'll be able to land by skidding the belly of his plane onto the runway; the bad news is that in doing so, the observation bubble will be crushed under the weight of the plane and his friend will die.

The rest of the drama focuses on the emotional tension of the pilot exhausting all other alternatives and coming to a dire realization: To save his crew and himself, landing the plane is his only option. If he doesn't try, they'll all die. Although it's unspoken, the other people also realize that landing will kill their friend under the plane. And the man in the observation bubble knows the same thing. This is where the story takes an unexpected turn.

In the next scene, we see the pilot in emotional agony as he begins the final approach for a landing and knows what's about to happen. Suddenly, the crewman in the observation dome drops into a trance. It's only then that we discover he's also an artist and has a sketch pad and pencil with him in his pack of supplies. We see him through the bubble as he quickly, expertly, and deliberately draws an image of the plane that he's in, complete with the observation dome and himself inside. Without a clue as to what's happening, we're left wondering why this guy is drawing a picture when his plane is about to crash.

With the plane sketched in perfect detail, the artist takes the liberty of putting one finishing touch on his creation—he draws the landing gear intact and fully extended, just as it would be if it were really there. But this isn't just any old landing gear he's drawn—it looks like huge, exaggerated doughnut tires, as if they were out of a *Mickey Mouse* cartoon. They're complete with candy-cane stripes and sparkling beams of light streaming from their surface.

The final stroke of the drawing is complete just as the plane touches the ground, and by this time the pilot is emotionally frazzled, believing that he's killing his friend. Well, you can imagine what happens next: As the pilot lands, he realizes that somehow the wheels are working. He maneuvers the plane to a stop. Immediately, the crew bolt from their places throughout the cabin, jump onto the tarmac, and begin running for safety.

As they turn around to determine how they were able to land, what they see is the reality of a fire-damaged, bullet-ridden, and war-battered plane—with cartoon tires holding it up and their friend from the observation bubble climbing down onto the runway to join them.

Here's the key to this story: Although the artist is conscious, he appears to be in a daze—what we today would call an *altered state*. He's in a waking dream. As long as he's dreaming, the make-believe tires are there, holding up the plane until everyone is safe. But as his comrades wildly hug him, they wake him from his "trance." We can see the plane in the background—suddenly the tires that he's imagining disappear from sight. They just vanish. The plane appears to hang in midair for a fraction of a second and then crashes to the ground in a cloud of smoke and fire, crushing the observation dome that he'd been strapped into only moments before. With disbelief, amazement, and wonder, the crew members look at one another and begin to cry—and that's where the story ends.

While this is a fictional account, it's powerful for two reasons:

1. First, it's a reminder that the very experience of imagination and belief that we're conditioned to discount in our culture is a creative force unto itself, one that lives within each of us and requires no special training other than knowing that it's there.

2. Second, this story reminds us that experiencing such a miracle in our lives requires that we *believe* in ourselves, as well as in the miracle itself.

While this story is a beautiful illustration of a possibility, the power of the artist's belief has a factual basis that we'll explore throughout the remainder of this book. The key is that he *believed* in the force of his imagination and *knew* that it had a direct link to the events in his life. In this example, rather than simply suspecting or halfway believing that he could rewrite his reality, he *knew* it with every fiber of his being.

He knew it so deeply that he somatized his belief, making the image in his dream the reality of his world. A growing body of scientific evidence suggests that we all have the power to do precisely that. I used the fictional story to open the door to the possibility, as it exhibits how multiple people, such as the plane's crew, can benefit from one individual's clarity even without understanding that power themselves. Perhaps most important, this story illustrates the innocence of the crewman in expressing his dream through his art. It shows just how simple the power of belief can be.

The following is a *true* account of these principles. It's the story of one woman's determination to succeed where no one had in the past and her belief that she would be the one to do it first.

### Real-Life "Miracles"

In 2005, Amanda Dennison of Alberta, Canada, was registered in *Guinness World Records* for the longest documented fire walk in history. While countless individuals have used such an experience as a confidence-building tool in personal-growth seminars, what made Amanda's walk a little different was how long she held the focus that allowed her to accomplish such a demonstration. On the day of her fire walk, she strolled through a bed of glowing coals averaging 1,700 degrees Fahrenheit, and she did so for a distance of 220 feet, to become the first person to set such a record without injury.[1]

There have been scientific theories offered in the past to explain how people have been able to walk uninjured on burning coals, covering much shorter distances. They include factors such as how fast the walker moves and the possibility that a thin film of perspiration on the feet insulates them from the glowing coals. Those theories simply don't hold up in the presence of the more than 200 feet of coals in Amanda's case. So what happened to her? What was it that set her apart from the people surrounding her on that summer day in 2005 and allowed her to perform such a feat?

Maybe the bigger question is: *What happens to _anyone_ who does something so miraculous?*

How many times have we heard of people doing things that seem to violate the common sense of everyday reality and even break the "laws" of physics and nature, at least as we understand them today? Televised newsmagazines, for example, have carried stories of soldiers returning from the battlefields of Iraq with injuries that their doctors say will prevent them from ever walking again. And then something happens—an inner experience that's not quite understood in medical terms—and a year later such people are running a marathon.

Or we hear of everyday people who suddenly have what appears to be a superhuman ability that they have never exhibited before—for example, the strength to save another person's life, as was the case of Tom Boyle of Tucson, Arizona, in the summer of 2006. After seeing a teenage boy struck by a car and then pinned beneath it, he ran to the scene and *lifted the car up high enough* for the driver to pull 18-year-old Kyle Holtrust out from under the vehicle.

Following the incident, Boyle offered an insight into his state of mind when he lifted the car. "All I could think is, what if that was my son?" he said. "I'd want someone to do the same for him, to take the time and rub his head and make him feel good until help arrived."[2] Although stories such as Boyle's are rare, they aren't unheard of. And we can't always attribute such feats solely to the strength of a man's body.

In the summer of 2005, *BBC News* carried the report of a woman who lifted over 20 times her body weight to free a friend who was trapped beneath her car following an accident—and she did so even though she was injured herself. The 5'7" woman, 23-year-old Kyla Smith, lost control of her car and it rolled over as it veered off the road. When it came to a rest, she could see that her friend's leg was outside the car, pinned beneath it. She pulled herself out of the driver's window and then *raised the car six or seven inches* from the ground to free her friend. "I just knew I had to set him free," she said following the accident, "and there was no one else around at the time."[3]

While these events don't occur every day, the point is that they *do* happen. And if they happen for one person, or a dozen people, then they may be the sign of something that's available to all of us. The key appears to be that we live our lives based on what we believe about our capabilities and our limits—for instance, that a car is too heavy for us to lift. It's only when something happens that changes us—such as another person depending on us for his or her life—that our limited beliefs change. Even if that lasts only for an instant, to understand what that "something" is, is to open the door to even greater possibilities of understanding ourselves and our world.

We owe it to ourselves and to one another to discover what changes occur within the people who can lift cars to rescue others or accomplish similar feats that reasoning says they can't. What is it about the way they think of themselves that makes them different from those around them who believe otherwise? Perhaps most important, how did a change in what they believed inside of themselves translate into a change in what they became capable of doing in the world?

To answer these seemingly innocent questions is to unlock what is perhaps the greatest secret of our existence. And to do so is to walk squarely into the fuzzy realm that has been the battleground of philosophers and religions for centuries and is now considered the last frontier of science: the mystery of consciousness and reality.

> **Belief Code 24:**
> A miracle that's possible for anyone is possible for everyone.

The crux of the mystery for both scientists and philosophers is that our everyday world doesn't appear to be the "real" one. Rather, we're living what's described as an illusion—what the ancients called a *shadow reality*—that is the reflection of something even more real than our everyday universe. The common thread that runs through each of these ideas is that the actual reality isn't here. It isn't even close to here. While our bodies are certainly in this world, the living force that expresses itself *through* them is actually based somewhere else, as a larger reality that we just can't see from our vantage point.

Historically, science has tended to discount such comparisons as "stories" created by nonscientific people to explain the things that they either don't understand or simply don't have any other explanations for . . . that is, until recently. Now, the existence of higher dimensions, the growing possibility that our world is a simulation, and the notion that consciousness is the stuff everything is made of is where scientific conversations begin! Whether we're looking at things from the perspective of science or spirituality, it still comes down to the same timeless question: *How real is our reality?*

### How Real Is "Real"?

When asked about his belief in reality, Albert Einstein often sounded more like a philosopher than a scientist in his reply. He's commonly quoted as stating that *reality is merely an illusion, albeit a very persistent one*—showing us that he suspected our everyday world might not be as certain as we would like to think.

In an address to the Prussian Academy of Sciences on January 27, 1921, he clarified his view of reality as a scientist. "As far as the laws of mathematics refer to reality, they are not certain," he began. Suggesting that we still don't know all there is to know about how the world works, he continued: "and as far as they [the laws of mathematics] are certain, they do not refer to reality."[4]

What a powerful and honest assessment of where we are in understanding the universe and our existence! In words that are simple and direct, the same mind that discovered how to release the energy of an atom ($E = mc^2$) was telling us that the explanation of how the universe works is still up for grabs.

In Mahayana Buddhism, the Lankavatara Sutra is considered to be one of the most important *sutras* (sacred texts).[5] It's believed to be the direct record of Buddha's words as he entered the great island of Ceylon, now Sri Lanka. Among the central keys of the text is the idea that there are no external objects in our reality. All that exists is consciousness. Within the consciousness of all that "is," both the world of form and the formless result from a special "subjective imagination."

So, while any experience certainly *seems* real enough to us, the teachings state that it's only where we direct our attention while we're having a feeling about the object of our focus that a possible reality becomes that "real" experience. In other words, what we experience as everyday reality is a form of collective dream.

Except for a slight variation in the language, this ancient tradition sounds a lot like the emerging theories of a virtual reality. In both the old and the new ways of thinking, we're intimately woven into the fabric of reality itself. In both, it's through our interaction while we're in the dream that the possibilities of our minds become the reality of our world. Rather than thinking of us as "outsiders" mysteriously dropped *into* the experience of our Earth reality, these traditions suggest that we're inseparable from it.

We get an idea of just how deep the interconnectedness between us and reality really goes if we think of the similar connection between a drop of water and the ocean where it's found. While it may be possible to separate the two under certain conditions, it's generally difficult to know where one ends and the other begins. For all intents and purposes, just as the ocean and the droplet are one and the same, we're part of the reality that we're creating.

What makes virtual reality and dream-time ideas so appealing are the unmistakable similarities between what they say about the way reality works. As mentioned in Chapter 1, for example, John Wheeler of Princeton University suggests that we not only play a role in reality, *but that we play a prime role* in what he calls a "participatory universe." As participants, we find that the act of focusing our consciousness—*of us looking somewhere and examining the world*—is an act of creation in and of itself. We're the ones looking. We're the ones who are examining our world. And everywhere we look, our consciousness makes something for us to perceive.

The common element that is key in all of these ideas is that in a participatory universe, you and I are part of the equation. We're simultaneously catalysts for the events of our lives as well as the experiencers of what we create. Both are happening at the same time.

As creators and experiencers, the question that begs to be asked is this: *If our interaction with the universe is constantly creating and modifying our world, then how do we know which interactions have which kind of effects? In other words, what are the rules that describe how our reality works? Do we have the wisdom to recognize them when we see them?*

> **Belief Code 25:**
> In a participatory reality, we are creating our experience as well as experiencing what we have created.

Or is it possible that we've already found them? Could the "laws" of physics be showing us the ins and outs of how reality plays out? If so, then as scientists solve the mysteries of nature, they're also showing us the spiritual keys to our own empowerment. To unlock it successfully, however, means that we must account for everything that we see as the rules are tested. This includes the anomalies—the things that don't always fit what the theories predict. As we often find, it's actually the anomalies that help us flesh out the subtle keys to the way things really work! This brings us to where we find ourselves today.

### Searching for the Rules of Reality

Over the last 300 years, scientists have proposed, tested, and updated their explanations of the universe and how things such as gravity and light work. The problem is that all of the effort has led to a place where we now have two sets of rules to describe what we see in different parts of the same reality: *classical physics* and *quantum physics.*

In 1687, Newton's "laws" laid the foundation for the science of classical physics. Along with James Maxwell's theories of electricity and magnetism from the late 1800s and Albert Einstein's theories of relativity from the early 1900s, classical physics has been tremendously successful in explaining the large-scale things that we see, such as the movement of planets and galaxies and apples falling from trees. It has served us so well that we are able to calculate the orbits for our satellites and even to put humans on the moon.

During the early 1900s, however, scientific advances showed us two places in nature where Newton's laws just don't seem to work: the very large world of galaxies and the very small one of quantum particles. Before that time, we simply didn't have the technology to watch the way atoms behave during the birth of a distant star or to peer into the subatomic universe. In both these large and small realms, scientists began to see things that couldn't be explained by classical physics.

Sometimes, for example, quantum energy shows itself as particles and acts just in the way particles are supposed to act. When it does, it follows the physical rules that scientists use to describe individual "things," the world seems right, and everyone is happy. At other times, however, quantum energy seems to defy those laws. It can appear in multiple places at the same time, communicate with the past from the present, and even change from a particle "thing" to an invisible wave of "non-things" to accommodate the situation. And this is the behavior that changes everything.

Because we're made of the same stuff that seems to violate the rules describing our world, its behavior also changes the rules that describe *us* and who we believe we are in the world. A new kind of physics—*quantum* physics—had to be developed that would explain these exceptions.

The difference in the way that the quantum and the everyday worlds seem to work has created two schools of thought among scientists. Each has its own theories to support it. The great challenge that remains is to marry these two different lines of thinking into a single view of the universe, a *unified* theory.

To do so requires the existence of something that connects the very large and the very small in ways that we're only beginning to understand. And that "something" has remained a mystery, even though we may have seen it as early as 1909.

### Does the World Change Because We're Looking?

While the idea that our beliefs and everyday reality are intimately connected is an old one, the scientific proof of the connection emerged suddenly with a single experiment performed one day in 1909. The demonstration itself is simple. The thinking that led to it is visionary. The results are so profound that we're still talking about them today.

In all probability, even the scientists who performed the now-famous double-slit experiment didn't know just how deeply their findings would affect their lives, the entire world, and the future of our planet. How could they? They were simply performing a scientific test exploring the "stuff" that everything is made of: the quantum particles of our bodies and the universe.

In his laboratory in England, physicist Geoffrey Ingram Taylor began his demonstration as he found a way to shoot the stuff that atoms are made of—quantum particles of light called *photons*—from a projector to a target a short distance away.[6] Here's the key: Before the photons could reach the target, they had to pass through a barrier that had two openings.

Just as water is able to travel through the many holes in a window screen when it thaws from ice to liquid, Taylor's experiment showed that the photons did something very similar. To the scientists' amazement, the photons changed from the particle form that could pass through one opening at a time in the barrier (the single slit), to a waveform that could pass through multiple openings in the barrier (the double slits). The reason why this is so mind-boggling is because there's absolutely nothing in conventional physics to account for how the stuff that everything is made of can change the very nature of its existence. To explain what they found, a new kind of physics had to be devised: *quantum physics.*

The two questions that Taylor and the scientists had to ask were: (1) "How did the particles 'know' that there was more than one opening in the barrier?" and (2) "What caused the particles to change into waves to accommodate the situation?" To answer these questions, they had to ask yet another, more revealing one: *"Who knew that there was more than one opening in the barrier?"* The answer is obvious— only those present in the room were aware of the precise conditions of the experiment: the scientists. The implication of this answer is where our ideas of reality are tested.

Could the "knowing" of the scientists have an effect on the experiment? Was it possible that the consciousness of the observers in the room—the belief and the expectation that the particles would behave in one way or another—somehow became part of the experiment itself? And if so, what does that mean for us? If the scientists' beliefs affected the photons in the experiment, then do *ours* do the same thing in everyday life?

This possibility opened the door to something that was almost unthinkable at the time. And the implications get very personal, very quickly. In the language of science, they suggest precisely what our most ancient and cherished spiritual traditions have stated is at the crux of our existence: The quality of our beliefs and expectations have a direct and powerful effect on what happens in our everyday life.

Nearly 90 years after it first shook the foundations of classical physics, the double-slit experiment was repeated. This time, however, the scientists had better technology and more sensitive equipment. In a report published in 1998 entitled "Quantum Theory Demonstrated: Observation Affects Reality," Israel's Weizmann Institute of Science confirmed the original 1909 experiments, while announcing an additional discovery that removed any doubt as to what the findings were demonstrating.[7] They found that the more the particles were watched, the more they were affected by the watcher.

> **Belief Code 26:**
> In 1998, scientists confirmed that photons are influenced just by being "watched" and discovered that the more intense the watching, the greater the watcher's influence on how the particles behave.

The 1998 experiment is important to our everyday lives because of the following undeniable facts:

- Our bodies and the world are made of the same quantum stuff that changed in the experiments when it was watched.

- We are all "watchers."

This means that the way we see the world and what we believe about what we see can no longer be discounted or written off as being of no consequence.

In fact, the experiments suggest that consciousness itself is what the entire universe is made of, and it may be the "missing link" in theories that would unify classical and quantum physics. John Wheeler leaves little doubt as to what the new experiments mean to him, stating: "We could not even imagine a universe that did not . . . contain observers [us] because the very building materials of the universe are these acts of observer-participancy."[8]

From our search to find the smallest particles of matter to our quest to define the edge of the universe, the relationship between observation and reality suggests that we may never find either. No matter how deeply we peer into the quantum world of the atom or how far we reach into the vastness of deep space, the act of our looking with the expectation that something exists may be precisely what creates something for us to see.

If so, then the prime rule that describes how our reality works may have already been revealed in Taylor's 1909 experiment.

### The Prime Rule of Reality

During a conversation with his student Esther Salaman around 1920, Albert Einstein revealed the "bottom line" with regard to his curiosity about God as a creative force in the universe. "I want to know how God created this world," he began. "I am not interested in this or that phenomenon, in the spectrum of this or that element. I want to know his [God's] thoughts. The rest are details."[9]

In many respects, our search for the rules that describe how our reality works are like Einstein's bottom line. While we can look for subtleties here and there, and they're useful when we find them, what we're really after is the key to how this world works. We want to know *how* and *why* things happen. Everything else is equivalent to Einstein's "details."

The original double-slit experiment and the variations on it that have been repeated have confirmed the basic premise of our most cherished spiritual traditions, which holds that the world around us is a mirror of our beliefs. From the ancient Indian Vedas, believed by some scholars to date to 5,000 B.C.E., to the 2,000-year-old Dead Sea Scrolls, a general theme seems to suggest that the world is actually the mirror of things that are happening on a higher realm, or in a deeper reality. Commenting on the new examinations of the Dead Sea Scroll fragments known as *The Songs of the Sabbath Sacrifice,* for example, its translators summarize the content: "What happens on earth is but a pale reflection of that greater, ultimate reality."[10]

The implication of both the ancient texts and quantum theory is that in the unseen worlds, we create the blueprint for the relationships, careers, successes, and failures of the visible one. From this perspective, our reality works like a great cosmic screen that allows us to see the nonphysical energy of our emotions and beliefs (that is, our anger, hate, and rage; as well as our love, compassion, and understanding) projected in the physical medium of life.

Perhaps this is why it's said that we hold the most powerful force in the cosmos from the instant of our birth—and that is the direct access to the universe. What could be more empowering than the ability to change the world and our lives simply by altering what we believe in our hearts and minds? Such a power sounds like the stuff of fairy tales. Maybe that's precisely why we're so drawn to such "fantasies": They awaken the memory that sleeps inside us of our power in the world and our ability to make reality the heaven or the hell that we choose.

If there's any doubt as to just how real this power is in our lives, we need look no further than the case histories of the placebo effect in Chapter 2, Amanda Dennison's fire-walking miracle at the beginning of this chapter, or the true-life account of a woman weighing little more than 100 pounds lifting a car that's at least 20 times her body weight. In the subconscious minds of those who experienced the placebo and performed the miraculous feats, and in the conscious mind of Amanda Dennison, we're shown the power of our ability to define our own limits of reality.

In each example, there's a direct correlation between what the person believed, how he or she felt about his or her beliefs, and what actually happened in the world. Although we may not fully understand *why* such effects work as they do, at the very least we must say that there *is* one. The unmistakable correlation that leads us to the prime rule of our reality is simply this: We must *become* in our lives what we choose to experience in our world.

Once we know this prime rule, the spiritual teachings of the past suddenly take on an even deeper, richer meaning. For me personally, I find myself in a place of even greater awe, respect, and gratitude for those in the past who did their very best to preserve this secret. In the words of their time, without the high-tech terms and experiments that prove what our 20th-century minds demand today, the

**Belief Code 27:**
The prime rule of reality is that we must *become* in our lives what we choose to experience in the world.

masters of our past shared the quantum secret of the greatest force in the universe. And, as we saw in the Dead Sea Scroll fragment cited previously, they did so in the presence of those who still believed that a rainstorm was the sign of angry gods!

Knowing that we must *become* in our lives the very things that we choose to experience in our world, the masters, healers, mystics, and saints of history demonstrated the prime rule in their miracles and healings. While many of those who were direct witnesses mistook the demonstrations as a sign of "specialness" and gave their power away to the one doing them, others recognized the gift that they'd been provided and passed the secret down to future generations.

They knew that we must give the stuff that reality is made of something to work with in order to perform a miracle. It makes perfect sense. If we expect reality (or God/the matrix/spirit/the universe) to answer our prayers, then we must *become* in our lives the template for the things that we're asking the atoms of reality to form. We've got to give the matrix something to work with. When we marry the prime rule with actions that allow it to serve us, something powerful and beautiful happens. And that "something" is what makes life so worthwhile!

### Living from the Answer

There's a subtle yet powerful difference between working *toward* a result and thinking and feeling *from* it.

When we work toward something, we embark upon an open-ended and never-ending journey. While we may identify milestones and set goals to get us closer to our accomplishment, in our minds we are always "on our way" to the objective, rather than in the experience of accomplishing it. The studies concluding "Observation affects reality" demonstrate two keys in translating the possibilities of our minds into the reality of our world:

1. Beyond any doubt, reality changes in the presence of our focus.

2. The more we focus, the greater the change.

These scientific observations confirm the principles that the great teachers of our past have shared in nonscientific language. And this is why Neville Goddard's admonition that we must "enter the image" (of our heart's desire, our dream, our goal, or our answered prayer) and "think from it" is so powerful. When we place our focus on what our lives would be like if our dreams were already fulfilled, what we're actually doing is creating the conditions within us that allow our fulfilled dream to surround us.

Let's take a look at Neville's work now.

Perhaps the best way to illustrate such a beautiful and profound truth is through an example. While the 20th-century philosopher known in his lifetime only as Neville shared many case histories that describe the "miracle" of living from an outcome, for me the following has been one of the most potent because of its simplicity, clarity, and innocence.

The story begins with Neville explaining the power of imagination and belief to a businesswoman who has come to see him for advice in New York. After he describes the philosophy of *living from the answer* and shares the instructions for how to do so, Neville's principles are validated in a way that even he wasn't expecting.

The woman's nine-year-old grandson was visiting her from out of state and had been with her during her meeting. As they were leaving the office, the young boy turned to Neville and stated excitedly,

"I know what I want, and now I know how to get it."[11] While both Neville and the woman were surprised by the boy's words, the philosopher asked the logical question: What was it that the boy was so clear about wanting? The answer that came next was no surprise to the boy's grandmother, as apparently the two of them had had this conversation many times in the past: He wanted a puppy. "Every night just as I'm going off to sleep I'm going to pretend that I have a dog and we are going for a walk," the boy said.

Adamant about all of the reasons why he *could not* have a dog, the woman explained to her grandson, once again, that his parents wouldn't allow it, that his father didn't even like dogs, and that the boy was just too young to care for one. There would be no dog, and that was it! . . . That is, until about six weeks later. It was then that the woman called Neville in amazement.

Following their day in the New York office, the boy had practiced everything he'd heard Neville and his grandmother discussing. While they'd believed he was playing with his toys during their conference, he had in fact been absorbing the specific details of their talk. Applying them each night as he drifted off to sleep, the boy imagined his new dog lying there in bed with him. The key here is that he felt himself in life *as if* the dog were already with him. In his beliefs, he lived his experience as though it were real. In his imagination, he "petted the dog actually feeling its fur."[12]

Ironically, not long afterward, the boy's school had a special contest in support of Kindness to Animals Week. Everyone in his class was asked to write an essay entitled "Why I Would Like to Own a Dog." After the entries were judged, the boy's won and he was awarded a beautiful young collie pup. After witnessing all of the synchronicities that led to their son having the puppy, the boy's parents recognized that something bigger than their feelings about the situation was taking place. They had a change of heart, and the boy's new friend was welcomed into their home.

While it's certainly possible to write this entirely off as coincidence, what comes next makes us stop and reconsider what this story is telling us. When the woman told Neville what had happened and described how her grandson had been awarded the collie puppy, the one thing she saved for last was the piece that tied everything together. Throughout all the time that her grandson had wished for a puppy, he'd been very clear about precisely what kind he wanted—it was always a collie!

One of the reasons why this story is so powerful is because of the way the young boy was able to grasp and apply the simple ideas that he'd overheard. In the course of a passing conversation that a stranger was having with his grandmother, he was able to separate Neville's philosophy from his grandmother's situation. While the adults were describing mature ideas applied to mature themes, he was able to glean the underlying principles that were meant to help his grandmother's business and apply them to his longing for a collie. If a child can do it, we all can! The key is for us to get out of our judgments and our beliefs about what is and isn't possible and allow the simplicity of the prime rule to unfold in our lives.

Although I'm constantly in awe when people share such compelling demonstrations of belief, seldom can I say that I'm truly surprised. After all, if belief were the most powerful force in the universe, then when a nine-year-old boy finds the puppy of his dreams in that universe—*the exact pet that he has imagined*—why would we expect anything different?

The secret here is that the boy was experiencing himself as if his puppy were already with him in his imagination. When he did, he was living *from* the outcome of his imagining. And in that outcome, his puppy was real. Using language that is direct and no-nonsense, the 19th-century psychologist and philosopher William James reminds us of just how easy it is to apply this principle in real life: "If you want a quality [in life], act as if you already had it. If you want a trait, act as if you already have the trait."[13] In Neville's words, the way to do this is to make "your future dream a present fact."[14]

To understand why something as simple as imagining that we're petting a dog, believing what we visualize, and "actually feeling its fur" is so powerful in our lives is to understand the very nature of our reflected reality. The poet William Blake recognized imagination as the essence of our existence, rather than something that we simply experience in our spare time. "Man is all Imagination," he said, clarifying, "The Eternal Body of Man is the Imagination, that is, God, Himself."[15]

Philosopher and poet John Mackenzie further described our relationship with the imagination, suggesting, "The distinction between what is real and what is imaginary is not one that can be finely maintained . . . all existing things are . . . imaginary."[16] In both of these descriptions, the concrete events of life must first be envisioned as possibilities before they can become a reality.

In nonscientific language, James, Neville, Mackenzie, and Blake each tell us precisely how we may apply the prime rule to real life. In our 21st-century world of microchips and nanotechnology, it's no wonder we're skeptical when we hear that moving the atoms of reality is so simple that even a child can do it. It just sounds too easy to be true . . . that is, until we consider what the science has shown us and what our most cherished spiritual traditions have always said: We live in a reflected universe, and we are creating the reflections.

So please don't be suspicious of the simplicity of Neville's words when he suggests that all we need to do to transform our imagination into reality is to "assume the feeling" of our wish fulfilled. In a participatory universe of our own making, why would we expect that the power to create should be any more difficult?

### A Rabbit with Antlers:
### Quantum Physics in a Buddhist Monastery

During my first journey into a Buddhist monastery in the late 1990s, I quickly discovered just how differently Western minds work from those of the monks and nuns in the places we'd come so far to explore. Without a doubt, the biggest difference was our seemingly endless need to know *why* things work the way they do and the *lack* of a need for that information in those living in the monasteries. They seemed to have an acceptance that sometimes things just "are" as they are. And it all appeared to be linked to what they believed of themselves and the world.

Following nearly two weeks of acclimating to altitudes as high as 16,000 feet above sea level, breathing the thick road dust that our ancient bus sucked into its ventilation system, and enduring 14-hour days of having our bodies bounced along roads that were little more than washed-out Jeep trails, I found my beliefs being tested in a way that I'd never expected.

We'd just arrived at a dilapidated monastery that was now occupied by a group of around 100 nuns. While we were sitting among them finishing a heartfelt sharing of sacred chants, the peace of the dimly lit room was suddenly shattered. As the door burst open, the harsh rays of the late-day sun made it impossible to see the face of the imposing silhouette standing in the entrance. In a voice that was just above a whisper, I heard our translator acknowledge the man in the doorway. "Geshe-la," he said, telling us that this was a powerful teacher.

While we were doing our best to see him, the man who commanded such authority made his way into the room to get a better look at *us*. When he did, I had my first opportunity to observe him. He was tall, his head was shaved, and he was definitely Tibetan. As he strolled slowly through the room, we remained seated on the thick mats that were used to insulate the nuns from the cold stone floor beneath. At first, the teacher said little as he looked over the room and evaluated the situation. Then he began shouting questions out loud to anyone who would answer.

I looked to our translator to understand what was happening, and he shared the conversation that was transpiring between the teacher and the nuns. "Who are these people?" the geshe asked as he made a sweeping motion over our heads with his hand. "What is happening in here?" He was obviously not used to a group of Westerners sitting with the nuns, doing what we were doing in the way we were doing it. Our translator joined the conversation as the nuns explained who we were and why we were there.

Then, just as abruptly as the man had come into the room, the tone of his questioning changed from one of suspicion and uncertainty to one of philosophy—specifically, the philosophy of what is real in the world. He asked the translator who the teacher of our group was, and suddenly all eyes were on me.

"Here!" our translator said, pointing in my direction. "Here is the geshe who has brought these people today." With barely a pause, the teacher then looked directly at me and asked me a question. Although I couldn't understand a word of his Tibetan dialect, I listened to the tone and inflection of his voice as our translator began to speak. "If you are on a pilgrimage in the desert and see a rabbit with antlers, is it real or is it imaginary?" he asked.

I couldn't believe what I was hearing. Here we were, just before sundown at a remote mountain monastery situated at 15,000 feet above sea level on the Tibetan plateau, with a roomful of chanting nuns, and this man was asking me about a "rabbit with antlers." When I was growing up, I'd heard of such a mythological creature, the impossible cross between a jackrabbit and an antelope—a jackalope—in the tall tales delirious hikers shared by campfire. While sightings of the jackalope seem to be abundant from North America to the Andes Mountains of Peru, I'd yet to be in the presence of anyone recounting the mystery who could do so with a straight face. Jackalopes simply don't exist. Yet here I was being quizzed about one in a place where I'd least expect it! As I was recovering from the surreal circumstances of the moment, I suddenly realized that this was a test and *I* was the one being tested.

Just as I was about to answer, I looked up at the teacher. The motion of his hands had created a small cloud of dust and lint as he gestured from beneath his robes. Suddenly the space around his imposing profile took on an eerie glow, almost like a halo, as the sun sparkled through the haze of suspended particles.

For some reason, my mind raced back to the question-and-answer format that I'd been taught in elementary school. After I was asked a question, I would repeat it in my own words to be sure that I'd understood it correctly. If so, I would then follow with my reply. "Is a rabbit with antlers in the desert real, or is it imaginary?" I began. All at once, even the nuns' typical chatter among themselves became very quiet. Everyone was listening for my answer to this impromptu philosophy quiz of reality. "The experience of the rabbit with antlers in the desert is the experience of the person who sees it," I began. "If that person is you, *it is as real as you believe it is."*

### Passing the Reality Test

The room was still as the words left my mouth. I held my breath, gazing up at the teacher to see if my answer was what he'd expected. He looked surprised. Slowly, a big grin spread across his face. As he turned to the translator, he asked another question. Then the translator grinned as he repeated the teacher's words.

"What monastery did this geshe come from?"

As the nuns heard this, there was a sigh of relief, followed by sporadic giggles that quickly led to a wave of laughter. Apparently my answer was typical of what might be expected from those who had learned of the revelations in the Buddhist scriptures; it wasn't one expected from a Westerner.

The teacher smiled as he turned and slowly walked back toward the door. The conversations in the room settled back into the low drone that had been present only moments earlier. Without a word, the monk stepped through the heavy brocaded cloths that keep the cold mountain air from blowing into the monastery. Feeling both a sense of honor at being asked the question and of accomplishment over the approval of my answer, we returned to our chants of peace.

Although my "test" had been brief, it was also a powerful confirmation of how widespread the knowledge of belief's power really is. What was so interesting about the exchange with our geshe was that his test confirmed both what the experiments are telling us and what the spiritual traditions of the world have suggested for centuries.

If the universe, our bodies, and everyday life are a virtual experience based on consciousness, then belief is the program that allows us to "wake up" while we're still in the simulation. So when we ask the age-old question "How real is reality?" the answer begins to sound like the solution to a philosophical riddle. *Reality is as real as we believe it is.* The secret is simply this: What we most identify with is what we experience in our lives. In this way, what we call our reality is soft, malleable, and subject to change. It conforms to our expectations and beliefs.

So while the "laws" of physics are certainly real enough and do exist under some conditions, the evidence suggests that when we change those conditions, we also rewrite the laws. And we don't have to be rocket scientists—or any scientists, for that matter—to do so. It can be as simple as Amanda Dennison walking on 1,700-degree coals or Milarepa pushing his hand *through* the native rock of a cave wall. In both instances, the laws of physics were violated. In each case, it was the ability of one individual to purposefully create the conditions of consciousness—what he or she believed to be true about his or her world—that changed the reality.

> **Belief Code 28:**
> We tend to experience in life what we identify with in our beliefs.

This is what brings science full circle back to the world's ancient mystical and spiritual traditions. Both science and mysticism describe a force that connects everything together. Both are saying that from within it, we each hold the power to influence how matter behaves, and reality unfolds, simply through the way in which we perceive the world around us.

Now that we know the prime rule of such a reflected reality, how do we apply it in our lives? If our deeply entrenched, sometimes-subconscious beliefs are the seed for what we experience, then how do we heal the false beliefs that limit us? How do we rewrite our reality code? This is where a new perspective that blows the conditions right off of everything we've held true in the past can be so powerful. The key is to find the experience that works for us—and to recognize it when it arrives.

CHAPTER SIX

# The Healing of Belief:
# How to Rewrite Your Reality Code

. . . . . . . . . . . . . . . . . . . . . . . . . . . . . . . . . . . . . .

*"The new way of seeing things will involve
an imaginative leap that will astonish us."*
— **John S. Bell** (1928–1990), quantum physicist

*"I see my life as an unfolding set of opportunities to awaken."*
— **Ram Dass,** philosopher

. . . . . . . . . . . . . . . . . . . . . . . . . . . . . . . . . . . . . .

In 1986, I attended a concert in Boulder, Colorado, and the headliner was a man who changed my life. His name was Michael Hedges, and he was arguably one of the most gifted guitarists of the 20th century.[1] In the summer of that year, he was on a rare solo tour that included the intimate venue where I met him.

Rather than the usual concert seating in a huge stadium where the artist looks like a speck on a distant stage, Michael chose to play in a casual restaurant setting. Pedestal tables were arranged around the stage, and no one was more than a few feet away from the performance. Everyone in the room could see everything, and see it very well.

Michael simply walked onstage, and, with little more than a "Hello, I'm Michael Hedges," something extraordinary began to happen: Suddenly his hands were doing things that I'd never seen a guitarist's do in my life. As he began his unaccompanied performance, his fingers stretched and bent in uncanny ways to form the chords and create sounds that gave the room a feeling that I can only describe as surreal. And not everything that happened was on the strings. Never missing a beat, the back and sides of his guitar became the percussion section for the taps and bumps that he was playing between the notes. What was even more amazing was that his eyes were closed throughout the whole concert!

I was so moved by what I'd seen that I strolled past his crew and walked right up to him during the intermission to thank him for such a powerful evening. Surprisingly, he greeted me as if he'd known me for years. He welcomed me to the stage, and together we walked to his instruments and he began asking me how certain effects sounded throughout the room. We chatted until the program resumed and I returned to my seat. I was absolutely enthralled by the rest of the show.

I never had the chance to speak with Michael Hedges again. While I felt that we probably would do so at some point in time, his sudden death in December 1997 prevented that from ever happening. Although my evening with him was brief, it was a life-changing experience.

I've been a guitarist since I was 11, and playing the instrument remains one of the most consistent passions of my life today. During the first six months when I was learning to play, I was indoctrinated into the form and style of *classical guitar.* The name says everything. There's a special posture that the body of a classical guitarist is taught to assume. The hands are positioned to hover over the strings but rarely touch the face of the instrument itself. While it's beautiful to watch in others, it always felt awkward and stiff to me.

The reason why I share this story is simply this: Watching Hedges that evening in 1986 forever changed the way I thought about playing a guitar. In the 90 minutes or so that he was onstage, he absolutely blew away all of the rules and any preconceived ideas of form and style that had been ingrained in me years earlier. It was so freeing for me to see him in his passion that it freed me in mine as well.

All that Michael Hedges had done was to share his gift. But in doing so, he became the living demonstration of a greater possibility. And that's the key to transforming what we believe to be true about our lives and our world. *To change the limitations of our personal pasts, our minds need a reason to change what we believe—and a good one at that.*

History is filled with examples of beliefs that were entrenched for hundreds or sometimes thousands of years and then changed overnight. History also describes what happens when the long-held ideas that support such beliefs are replaced by something so radical that an entire worldview suddenly topples and falls. Sometimes the changes are small and seemingly insignificant, such as watching a guitarist for 90 minutes on the stage. Occasionally they're so huge that they forever transform the way we think of ourselves and the universe.

In the summer of 2006, for example, 2,500 scientists gathered in Prague, Czech Republic, for the general assembly of the International Astronomical Union (IAU). Due to the discovery that there are other chunks of rock even larger than Pluto orbiting our sun, the former planet was reclassified as a dwarf planet. It happened just like that! One minute Pluto was a real planet; the next, it wasn't. While this reclassification surprised and saddened some people, in the overall scheme of our lives it had little impact. Beyond the fact that all astronomy books written before 2006 are now obsolete, Pluto's new designation probably hasn't really rocked anyone's world.

In 1513, however, another astronomical discovery made us aware of a single fact that forever changed our view of the universe and, ultimately, ourselves. It was in that year that Nicolaus Copernicus, a lawyer studying astronomy in his spare time, devised his calculations proving that the sun, not the Earth, is the center of our solar system.

While the idea had been proposed more than 1,700 years earlier by the Greek astronomer Aristarchus of Samos, it was considered so outrageous that the philosophers and astronomers of his time created "reasons" to discredit what he'd found.

 ᴨ example of a belief that *did* change our lives, and did so
  ᴨat continues to this very day. When Copernicus's book *De
  nibus Orbium Coelestium* was finally published after his death
   3, everyone from the leaders of the Roman Catholic Church
downᴨ to the average person on the street had to adjust their way of
thinking to make room for a sun-centered *solar system* (even that term
is part of the change that took place). Like Michael Hedges, all Copernicus did was share his knowledge.

The key in both of these instances is that the belief regarding an
established way of seeing things was changed, seemingly overnight.
And it was done through the inarguable demonstration of another
possibility.


### Rewriting Our Reality Code

At the turn of the last century, a great philosopher stated: "The
world we see that seems so insane, is the result of a belief system that
is not working."[2] While this sounds like something we'd expect to hear
from a self-help teaching at the dawn of our new millennium, it was
actually uttered by William James at the end of the 19th century. In
just a few words that are as meaningful for the changes we see today
as they were for those during his time, James implied the theme, and
the intent, of this book.

If the world that "seems so insane" is based in our perceptions,
then why is it so hard for us to change the things that don't work?
How do we rewrite our beliefs to reflect our deepest loves, truest
desires, and greatest means of healing?

*To rewrite our reality code, we must give ourselves a reason to
change what we've believed in the past.* The message of this sentence
is both plainly obvious and deceptively simple. It's obvious because
of the undeniable relationships between belief and reality described
throughout this book. You may be saying to yourself, "Of course all it
takes to change our world is a change in what we believe." But in the
simplicity of what's so straightforward comes the catch.

Changing our beliefs may be the most difficult thing that we do in life. *It's more than just a matter of making up our minds to change, or having the will to do so.* Much more.

The reason is because of what we think our beliefs say about us. Geoff Heath, former principal lecturer in counseling and human relations at the University of Derby in England, describes the crux of our dilemma: "We are what we come to believe ourselves to be. To change our beliefs is to change our identities. . . . That's why it's difficult to change our beliefs."[3] What Heath is saying here goes a long way toward answering the question of why it's so hard for us to modify our perceptions.

For the most part, we've grown comfortable with ourselves and the way we see our world. The proof is that if we weren't, we'd be constantly searching for new reasons to change our lives. To upset our comfort zone is to shake the very foundation that allows us to feel safe in the world. So to make a change in something as powerful as the core beliefs that define our lives, we need a trigger that's equally powerful. We need a *reason* to jolt us from the complacency of one way of thinking into a new, and sometimes revolutionary, way of seeing things. In short, we need a different perspective.

The catalyst for a new perspective may be something as simple as connecting the dots of newly discovered facts that lead to a novel understanding that simply makes sense. Or it may take something that blows the doors right off of everything we've believed in the past to catapult us into a greater possibility—something like a real-life miracle!

Both logic and miracles give us good reasons to see the world differently. While the latter have been used by the great masters of our past, the discoveries of today's science are opening the door to entirely new ways of seeing the world without miracles. And that's why considering the universe as a computer and belief as a program is so powerful. Because we already know how both work, when we look for a way to change, it gives us a familiar place to begin.

### *Is Hurt a Glitch in Belief?*

After leaving the corporate world in 1990, I was living temporarily in the San Francisco area developing seminars and writing books by day. In the evenings I would work with clients who had asked for my help in understanding the role of belief in their lives and relationships. One evening I scheduled an appointment with a client whom I'd worked with many times before.

Our session began as usual. As the woman relaxed into the wicker chair in front of me, I asked her to describe what had happened in the week since we'd last talked. She began telling me about her relationship with her husband of 18 years. For much of the marriage they'd fought, sometimes violently. She had been on the receiving end of daily criticism and invalidation of everything from her appearance and dress to her housekeeping and cooking. This belittling found its way into every aspect of their lives, including the moments of intimacy that had grown increasingly rare over the years.

What made the past week different was that the situation had escalated to a point of physical abuse. Her husband had become angry when she confronted him with questions about his "overtime" and late nights at the office. She was miserable with the man she'd loved and trusted for so long. Now, that misery was compounded by the danger of bodily harm and emotions that were out of control. After knocking her across the room in their most recent fight, her husband had left to live with a friend. There was no phone number, no address, and no indication of when, or even if, they would see each other again.

The man who had made my client's life such hell through years of emotional abuse and now potentially life-threatening violence was gone at last. As she described his departure, I was waiting for some sign of her relief—a sign that never appeared. In its place, however, something astonishing happened: She began to weep uncontrollably with the realization that he was gone. When I asked how she could miss someone who had hurt her so much, she described herself as feeling "crushed" and "devastated" by his absence. Rather than embracing her husband's leaving as an opportunity to live free of abuse and criticism, in her state of mind it felt like being sentenced to a lifetime of loneliness. She felt that it was better to have her husband in the house, even with the abuse, than to have no one there at all.

I soon discovered that my client's situation wasn't unique or even unusual. In fact, after talking with others in the self-help industry, I found it was just the opposite. When we find ourselves in situations where we give ourselves away—our power, our self-esteem, our self-confidence—it's not surprising to experience precisely what my client was feeling and to cling to the very experiences that hurt us the most. My question was "Why?"

How does so much suffering and hurt find its way into our lives? Why do we hold fast to damaging beliefs, in essence perpetuating the very experiences that we'd like to heal? When we ask these questions, could it be that we're really asking something even more basic? The beliefs that bring the pain and suffering are examples of a limited way of seeing the world. So maybe the real question is: *Why do we cling to the beliefs that limit us in life?*

Our metaphor of belief as a program may offer a clue. If we had a computer program that hurt us every time we pushed the "on" button, just as our beliefs sometimes do, we'd say that it wasn't working properly—that it had an error. So do the beliefs that we feed into the mirror of consciousness have a defect that leads us to perpetuate the experiences that hurt us? Or is it possible that the program itself works impeccably and it's the way in which we're using our beliefs that's signaling the need for change?

Regardless of how expertly a computer program is put together or how professional the programmers are, there's always the possibility that it will malfunction at some point. And when it does, the malfunction is called a *bug,* a *hiccup,* or more commonly, a *glitch.* If our world is really a simulation created by a sophisticated computer, then could the program that has created it ever have a problem? Could the consciousness computer of the universe ever have a glitch? And if so, would we know it if we saw it?

In his 1992 paper "Living in a Simulated Universe," John Barrow explored this very question, stating: "If we live in a simulated reality, we might expect to see occasional glitches . . . in the supposed constants and laws of Nature over time."[4] While this kind of problem is certainly possible, it could be that we're already experiencing another type of glitch, perhaps one that even the architect of our reality never expected.

Having a glitch doesn't always mean that the program was written incorrectly. In fact, it may run perfectly under the conditions for which it was originally designed. Sometimes, however, a program made for one condition finds itself in a very different set of circumstances. Although it still does what it was always intended to do—and does it really well—in another environment it may not produce the expected outcome, so it looks as if the program has an error.

This leads us to a question: In the programs of consciousness, are hatred, fear, and war the result of a glitch in our beliefs? While the quantum stuff of the universe definitely reflects what we believe, is it possible that we were never meant to focus our beliefs on the things that hurt us in life? How have we come to feel so alone in a world that we share with more than six billion of our kind? Where did we learn to experience so much fear, and why do we allow our fears to become so deeply ingrained in our beliefs that they ultimately make us sick? If these are the glitches in our consciousness, can we fix them in the way we would a program glitch?

### Fixing the Beliefs That Hurt Us

In much the same way that skateboarders, musicians, and coffee aficionados have their own lingo to describe their passions, computer programmers have always had a special language that they use in private conversations about their craft. Thanks to high-tech movies of recent years, many of the terms that were once shared only in the privileged inner circles of software "techies" have become commonplace in our lives. We all know what it means, for example, when someone tells us that we have a "bug" in our program, or that our system has "crashed."

Programmers even have a special word they use for the commands that *fix* problems in existing software. Collectively, the commands are called just that: a *fix*, or a *software patch*, or sometimes simply a *patch*. The bottom line here is that this is a small piece of code inserted into the original software that solves a problem. Whether we're aware of it or not, software patches play a powerful role in our lives.

At the turn of the 21st century, for example, it was a patch that saved us from the worst-case scenario of what could have been the Y2K disaster. From global power grids and satellites to cell phones and the early-warning defense systems that protect North America, all were dependent upon date codes that were set to "expire" at midnight on the last day of the year 1999. For each system that would be affected, a small program was made available to users that would allow for a smooth transition from dates that began with the "19" of the 1900s to those that began with the "20" of the 2000s—the Y2K patch. As they say, the rest is history. The patch worked, and our software will tide us over until new programs are developed or the year 2100 arrives, whichever comes first.

The point is simply this: Could something similar be happening to us right now? And if so, can we fix our glitch? Can we rewrite the beliefs that may have limited us in the past?

### Using Logic and Miracles to Change Our Beliefs

In Chapter 3, we explored the two places where we keep the beliefs that hurt—as well as heal—our lives: the conscious and subconscious minds. To heal the limits of either a conscious or subconscious perception, we must somehow bypass what the mind has believed in the past and replace it with something new based in an experience that's true for us: our inarguable truth.

For thousands of years, miracles have done precisely this. While they're still just as powerful today as in the past, many people believe that they've become hard to find. Although this may or may not be the case, depending on how we see the world, now we can also use the power of logic to speak directly to our conscious minds. And when we consciously accept a new way of seeing the world, our subconscious beliefs are affected as well.

Building upon the computer analogies that we've used in previous chapters, replacing an existing belief in the conscious mind with a new, upgraded, and improved one may be thought of in the same way we've thought of a software patch. The patch is built independently of the original software and inserted at a later time to upgrade the program and "heal" it from unwanted responses. History has shown that both logic and miracles can become the superhighway to the deeply held beliefs that our minds have accepted in the past.

Let's take a closer look at the logic patch and the miracle patch to see what they are and how to create them:

— **Logic Patch:** We can convince our conscious minds of a new belief through the power of logic. Once the mind sees a reason to think differently about the world, it will allow the heart to embrace that possibility as a new belief—that is, to feel that it is true.

> **Belief Code 29:**
> For different reasons that reflect the variations in the way we learn, both logic and miracles give us a way into the deepest recesses of our beliefs.

— **Miracle Patch:** We can bypass the logic of our minds altogether and go directly to our hearts. In this way, we don't even need to think about what we believe. We're forced to embrace a new belief in the presence of an experience that's *beyond* rational explanation. This is the definition of a miracle.

When we talk about changing a belief consciously, one of the most powerful things we can do is become aware of it and how it plays out as the subconscious habits of our daily routines. To embark upon such a path is to hold the focus of conscious intent for everything we do in every moment of life. In the Buddhist traditions, this practice of mindfulness, called *Satipatthana,* was recommended by Buddha for all who seek to grow spiritually and eventually attain enlightenment. In our world today, however, it may not be practical to focus our awareness on each task of every moment to make the changes in our beliefs. And, as we saw earlier, we don't have to.

If we want to identify what our true beliefs are, we need look no further than the world around us to see their reflections in our relationships, careers, abundance, and health. If we hope to change those things, we need a way to transcend the limits of the beliefs that created them. From the viewpoint of beliefs as programs, this is where the miracle patch and the logic patch come in.

### The Logic Patch

For a logic patch to work, the mind needs to see a flow of information that leads us to a logical conclusion—one that makes sense to us. If we can see the connection in our minds, then the questioning steps aside and allows our hearts to accept what we're shown. In other words, we believe it.

In some branches of mathematics there are statements (proofs) in the form of "If this . . . then that" to lead to just such a conclusion. For example, we may say something like this:

**If:** Water at room temperature is wet.
**And:** We are covered in water at room temperature.
**Then:** We are wet.

In the preceding statements, we're presented with two facts with which our minds can't argue: (1) We *know* beyond any reasonable doubt that water at room temperature is wet—and it's *always* wet; and (2) we also *know* that if we're covered in water at room temperature, we'll be wet as well.

Discounting any extenuating circumstances, such as being under an umbrella or wearing a raincoat, our minds easily make the connection. It's obvious to us that *if* we're covered in water, *then* we're going to be wet. While this may be a silly example, the point is clear. It's all about connecting facts.

> **Belief Code 30:**
> To change our beliefs through the logic of our minds, we must convince ourselves of a new possibility through inarguable facts that lead to an inescapable conclusion.

Now, using a similar way of thinking, let's apply this kind of logic to our role in the universe. I invite you to consider the following:

**If:** We are capable of imagining anything in our minds.

**And:** The power of our deepest belief translates what we imagine into what is real.

**Then:** We can "fix" the limiting glitch in our beliefs and thereby relieve the greatest suffering in our lives.

In other words, we can create the "patch" in our beliefs that would make the limitations of the past obsolete. When the glitch is fixed, the old belief is replaced by a new and powerful reality. This is precisely what we've seen in a number of instances looked at in this book, including:

- My friend's husband who healed the generations-old expectation that he would die at the age of 35

- Amanda Dennison's belief that she would walk safely over more than 200 feet of burning coals

- People who lifted automobiles from the ground long enough to free those pinned beneath them

- The boy in Neville's office who wanted a collie puppy

One way we apply the logic patch in our lives is when we see another person accomplish something that we believed impossible. Although there may be no "logical" reason *why* we can't do something, if no one has done it before, a seemingly difficult feat can create such a strong belief in our minds that we begin to believe that it's impossible . . . that is, until someone proves us wrong.

### One Person's Logic Is Another Person's Miracle

The first records for the one-mile run considered accurate by today's standards weren't kept until the mid-1800s. It was during that time that modern running tracks were built following strict guidelines that would assure the accuracy of the distance and provide a consistent surface for the runners who were competing. On July 26, 1852, Charles Westhall established the modern benchmark for the one-mile run at the new track built on the Copenhagen House Grounds in London. His time was a blazing 4 minutes and 28 seconds, setting a record that would not be bested for a long time by footracing standards: another six years.

While Westhall's original record would be broken at least 31 times throughout the late 1800s and early 1900s, on each occasion the new record was just slightly better than the previous one, sometimes by only fractions of a second. All were still over four minutes, the time that seemed like the human limit to run a mile. For more than 100 years, although many people did try, it was thought—*it was believed*— that humans simply weren't physically capable of covering one mile on foot in anything less than four minutes . . . that is, until 1954, when the seemingly impossible happened.

On May 6 of that year, British runner Roger Bannister broke the elusive four-minute barrier for the very first time in recorded human history. On a track in Oxford, England, he covered the mile in 3 minutes and 59.4 seconds. And here is where the story fits into the power of our beliefs.

Although it had taken 102 years for Bannister to break the four-minute-mile mark, *fewer than eight weeks later it was broken again* by John Landy of Australia, with a time of 3 minutes and 57.9 seconds. Once the seemingly impossible limit of the four minutes was broken, it shattered the belief that it couldn't be done and opened the door for others to follow with times that were even faster. Since Roger Bannister's feat in 1954, the record for the one-mile run has been broken at least 18 times, with the record now held by Moroccan runner Hicham El Guerrouj for his 1999 run of 3 minutes and 43.13 seconds! Once it was clear in consciousness that the four-minute mile was no longer a limit of fact, the beliefs of others were freed to discover what *new* limits might look like. We continue to push them today.

To those who were convinced that four minutes was the fastest a human could ever run the mile, Bannister's record-breaking time was a miracle. Because in more than a century it hadn't been done, the critics of any attempt to break that record believed that it was simply impossible to do so. To Bannister, however, his achievement wasn't a miracle; it was the end product of the logic and deduction that convinced him that it *could* be done. So, in an interesting twist, the logical process of one person planning and working toward a goal can seem like a miracle to others. As this example shows us, it takes only one person to demonstrate that something is possible and that individual's miracle can give us all the unconscious permission to duplicate it.

So how did Bannister do it? While only Bannister himself will ever know *precisely* what was going through his mind to free him from the limit of the existing records, we do know that he used logic to set his professional goals and change his personal beliefs. First, he chose a goal that was clear and precise. It's rumored that during his training he slipped a piece of paper into his shoe inscribed with the exact time that he chose to run: 3 minutes and 58 seconds.

He approached his goal using logic to convince his mind that it was attainable. As opposed to looking at the entire record as an obstacle, he chose to think of it in terms of being only mere seconds faster than another time he'd already accomplished. If we were to do the same thing today, using our preceding model, the logic would look something like this:

**If:** I can already run a mile in 4:01.

**And:** All I need to do is run one second faster than I have run already to tie the record at 4:00.

**And:** All I need to do is run one second faster than that to set a new record at 3:59.

**Then:** I can do that! I can run just two seconds faster than I already do.

In this example, when we think of things in this way, it makes big goals seem more accessible. Rather than considering the totality of the world record; the entire project in the office; or everything that it takes to change jobs, move to a new city, and begin a new career, we seem to do better if we can set our goals in small increments, with each one getting us just a little closer to our ultimate objective.

When we apply this idea as a "logic patch" to our personal beliefs, it helps us bypass the old ideas that may have kept us from achieving our greatest dreams and loftiest aspirations. Whether it's running the fastest mile in the world, organizing the wedding of the century, or switching careers in the middle of life, if we're going to convince ourselves that it can work, we need to understand how the mind operates and honor what it needs in order for our change to be successful.

### Building Your Personal Logic Patch

Following is a template that you can use to build a logic patch for yourself. What sets this process apart from an affirmation is that here you're stating your own facts, based upon your personal experience, which lead you to a logical and inarguable conclusion. Just as in the earlier examples, the key is to be clear, honest, and concise so that the patch will make sense to your mind.

**Key 1: State how you feel regarding your desired outcome as if it has already happened. For your own clarity, it's important to do this in one concise, brief sentence.**
*Example:* I feel deeply fulfilled by the success of my new business teaching sustainable living.

I feel _____.

**Key 2: State which passion you are choosing to express.**
*Example:* I have a passion to create and to share what I've created.
*Example:* I have a passion to help others.

I have a passion to _____.

**Key 3: State the limiting belief(s) that you have about yourself and/or filling your need.**

*Example:* My limiting belief is that my work is not worth the time it takes to create.

*Example:* My limiting belief is that my work is insignificant.

*Example:* My limiting belief is that my family demands don't allow me to fulfill this need.

My limiting belief is that _____.

**Key 4: State the opposite of your limiting belief(s).**

*Example:* My work makes a meaningful contribution to my life and the world.

*Example:* My work is valuable.

*Example:* My family wants me to be happy and supports me in my choices.

My _____.

**Key 5: State when you feel most fulfilled in life. This will become your goal.**

*Example:* I feel most fulfilled in life when I think of writing a new book about sustainable living.

*Example:* I feel most fulfilled in life when I'm creating workshops to teach "green" living.

I feel most fulfilled in life when _____.

**Key 6: State the inarguable fact(s) that support your goal.**

*Example:* It is a fact that there's a demand for new books teaching sustainable living.

*Example:* It is a fact that I've already practiced a green lifestyle for 25 years.

*Example:* It is a fact that I'm already teaching other people about this informally.

*Example:* It is a fact that new technology makes it possible to be more efficient.

*Example:* It is a fact that I express myself well in writing and I've already written brief articles on this topic.

It is a fact that _____.

While Roger Bannister may not have sat down and gone through the formalities that I'm describing here, we know that he did use a step-by-step process of logic to prove to himself that his goal could be accomplished and that he was the person to do it. And this is the key to a logic patch. It needs to make sense to you—and only you—by proving to you that your goals, dreams, and desires are valuable and achievable.

With these things in mind, and using the information from the questions above, complete the following chart to create your personal logic patch. Because you can include as many statements as you choose for Keys 4, 5, and 6, your personal logic patch can contain an unlimited number of "And" statements.

| Template for Your Personal Logic Patch | |
|---|---|
| **Logic Statement** | **Key Number** |
| **If:** | 2 |
| **And:** | 5 |
| **And:** | 6 |
| **Then it makes sense that:** | 4 |
| **And I have all that I need to bring my dream to life.** | |

Using the preceding examples, your finished logic statements will look like the following:

**If:** I have a passion to create and to share what I've created.

**And:** I feel most fulfilled in life when I think of writing a new book about sustainable living.

**And:** I feel most fulfilled in life when I'm creating workshops to teach "green" living.

**And:** It's a fact that there's a demand for new books teaching sustainable living.

**And:** It's a fact that I've already practiced a green lifestyle for 25 years.

**And:** It's a fact that I'm already teaching other people about this informally.

**Then it makes sense that:** My work makes a meaningful contribution to my life and the world, my work is valuable, and my family wants me to be happy and supports me in my choices.

**And I have all that I need to bring my dream to life.**

This template is a blueprint to organize your beliefs into statements that are true for you and can't be dispelled. The blueprint is just that—it's a place to begin. It represents a tried-and-true progression of thoughts—a powerful sequence of information—that will give you a reason to change a deeply held belief. The important thing to remember when using this template is simply this: Its purpose is to create a program for yourself . . . for your beliefs. The key is that *you* provide the information that's meaningful to *you,* and, in that way, you're accessing *your* subconscious mind. Because we each work a little differently, your program might not be effective for someone else.

While a logic patch can be a powerful tool, sometimes we require more than simple logic to change our deepest beliefs on a conscious level. We need more than the reasoning of "If" and "Then" statements in our minds to free us from an existing belief, possibly because the one that we're trying to heal is so close to us, so personal, that we just can't be objective.

I've often found this to be true for myself when I'm with a friend or family member in a life-and-death situation. Regardless of what all of the facts, statistics, and reasoning tell my mind, my instinct is that I just want those I love to be "okay." I desire for them to be safe, comfortable, and well. In such moments, the logic just doesn't work.

This is when it's best to go directly to the one place in our bodies that was designed to create the belief waves that change our world. We need to speak directly to the heart, and logic isn't going to do it. That's when we need a really good miracle!

### The Miracle Patch

Perhaps it was Neville who best described our power of belief to transcend the limits of our past. From his perspective, all that we experience—*literally everything that happens to us or is done by us*—is the product of our consciousness and absolutely nothing else. Up until his death in 1972, he shared the keys of using imagination and belief to open the door of the miracles of our lives.

From Neville's perspective, the miracle is the outcome itself. By its very nature, it describes a situation that has already happened. While miracles are often associated with the reversal of disease and are certainly welcome when they appear in that form in our lives, they aren't limited to physical healings.

The definition of a miracle is that it is "an event that appears inexplicable by the laws of nature."[5] This is where we find its power. It's *beyond* the logic of where it comes from or how it happened. The fact is that it *did* happen. And in its presence, we are changed. Although different people may be affected in different ways, when we experience something that we can't explain, it gives us pause. We must reconcile that miracle with what we've believed to be true in the past.

The morning light peeked from behind the mountains and suddenly the desert came alive. In the first rays of the early sun, I could see the faces of the young Egyptian soldiers, our military escort, staring back into our tour bus from the lead truck in our convoy. Five or so men were seated on makeshift benches lining either side of the truck bed, their job to escort us safely across the Sinai Desert into the huge city of Cairo.

Nearly as fast as the Egyptian weather seemed to change, the local political situation had become tense during our time in the mountains. Now for our overland route back to the hotel, a checkpoint system had been set up for our safety and to establish our whereabouts at all times. I knew that it would be only a matter of minutes before we would slow to a stop, a guard would step onto the bus to check our papers, he'd say *Shukran* ("Thank you"), and we'd be on our way.

After clearing the first series of checkpoints, we soon found ourselves winding our way along the brilliant white beaches of the Red Sea toward the Suez Canal. In the warmth of the late-morning sun pouring through our sightseeing coach, I closed my eyes and imagined the same scene more than 3,000 years ago as the people of Egypt traveled a similar route to the mountain from which we were now returning. Except for the buses and the paved roads, I wondered how much had really changed. I soon found myself in conversation with members of our group, anticipating our entrance into the ancient chambers of the Great Pyramid scheduled for later that evening in Cairo.

Suddenly, everything stopped. I looked up as our bus came to a halt along a busy boulevard. From my seat just behind the bus driver, I peered through the windows, looking for familiar landmarks to orient myself. To my amazement, we were stopped in front of a monument that is one of the most powerful symbols in all of Egypt, perhaps even more powerful than the pyramids themselves: the tomb of former president Anwar el-Sādāt.

As I stood up to speak with our guide and find out why we were stopped, I could see the activity in the street outside our bus. The soldiers had jumped out from under the canopies of their troop carriers and were milling around with their superiors and our driver. As I hopped down from the steps of the bus onto the street, immediately I noticed that something wasn't business as usual. The soldiers, our driver, and our Egyptian guide all had puzzled expressions on their faces. Some were tapping their wristwatches and holding them to their ears to see if they were running. Others were anxiously shouting to one another in short bursts of Egyptian.

"What's happening?" I asked our guide. "Why have we stopped here? This isn't our hotel!"

He looked at me in absolute awe. "Something isn't right," he said with a rare intensity in his normally playful voice. "We shouldn't be here yet!"

"What are you saying?" I asked. "This is *precisely* where we should be: on our way to our hotel in Giza."

"No!" he said. "You don't understand. We *cannot* be here yet! It hasn't been long enough since our departure from St. Catherine's Monastery in Sinai for us to be in Cairo. It takes at least eight hours for us to make the drive under the Suez Canal, across the desert, and into the mountains. *At least eight hours.* With the checkpoints, we should arrive even later. Look at the guards—even they don't believe their eyes. It's been only four hours. Our being here is a miracle!"

As I watched the men in front of me, an eerie feeling swept over my body. Although I'd had experiences similar to this one when I was alone, it had never happened with an entire group. Following a troop carrier and observing the speed limits—and with the extra time at the checkpoints—how could our driving time have been cut in half? Although the distance between Cairo and St. Catherine's hadn't changed, our experience of time while we traveled it did. It was a fact that was recorded on the wristwatches of every military man, armed guard, and passenger on our bus. It was as if our memories of the day had somehow been squeezed into an experience of half the duration we expected. Where had the rest of the time gone? What had happened, and why? The conversations that were taking place on the bus during the drive may offer a clue.

I mentioned that our group was scheduled for a private entrance into the Great Pyramid later in the evening. For many people, it would be the highlight of the trip, and it had been the topic of conversation since we began our morning. In the innocence of anticipating the experiences that were yet to come, the group was talking about them as if they had already happened—as if they were already inside of the king's chamber of the Great Pyramid. They were talking about what sounds they'd utter in the acoustically perfect room, how the air would smell, and what it would feel like to be inside the monument that they'd seen in movies and documentaries since they were children.

The key to our mystery is this: In the belief of the group, they were already inside of the Great Pyramid. Just as Neville had described in his conversation with the young boy's grandmother, they were assuming the feeling of their wish fulfilled. In doing so, they shifted their focus from how long the bus trip would take to what it was like to be in the pyramid. On that day, with 60 or so people all sharing a common feeling, their reality changed to reflect it. Interestingly, even those who weren't actively participating in the experience—the soldiers, the drivers, and the guides—shared in the benefit of what was created.

There's no scientific reason to explain why travelers on a journey that would normally take a full day could cover the same distance in half the time. And that's the definition of a miracle: It's an event that appears inexplicable by science (as least as we know its laws today).

I'm sharing this story for two reasons.

1.  First, I want to illustrate that a miracle can be experienced alone or with a group. Either way, everyone can participate in the same "group dream" and experience the same outcome.

2.  Second, this story demonstrates that the group miracle can happen spontaneously, just as we've seen. There was no conscious effort on the part of the people on the bus to make us "go faster" or "get to Cairo more quickly." On the contrary, in the minds of those excited about the evening to come, they were already there. As they accepted their experience *as if it were already happening,* their reality of time shifted to accommodate their experience.

The beauty of this miracle is that no one had to understand the physics of time warps, wormholes, and quantum energy for it to happen. I believe that reality always works just this way and changes just this easily.

In terms of our miracle patch, what's important here is that our group experience wasn't the result of a mental process of logic. We didn't go through all of the reasons that may have led to a long trip or try to convince our driver to take a shortcut. We didn't have to understand *why* it worked in order for it to do so. In fact, this story beautifully illustrates that it's less about making something happen and more about believing that it already *has.*

Riding on our bus that day, we simply abandoned ourselves to the feeling and belief that we were already in the place we'd waited a lifetime and traveled halfway around the world to see. And maybe that's all it takes to wrinkle space and time and to breathe life into our dreams on a regular basis. This is why the miracle patch can be so powerful—it allows us to participate in our reality for reasons we don't necessarily recognize and may never understand.

> **Belief Code 31:**
> The power of a miracle is that we don't have to understand *why* it works. We must, however, be willing to accept what it brings to our lives.

Whether we see a miracle in another's life or it happens to us personally, what's important here is that either way, we experience something that's beyond reasoning. When we do, our conscious minds and, ultimately, our beliefs are changed. In the presence of our acceptance that the miracle "is," all that can happen is the miraculous. So the key to using a miracle to change our beliefs is to find the miraculous events that already exist in our own lives and teach ourselves to recognize them when we see them.

Miracles mean different things to different people. For some, witnessing an event that's beyond anything they can explain causes them to feel "less than" and insignificant in their lives. Because their subconscious conditioning has already led them to feel powerless in the world, they may be predisposed to giving their power to others.

So whether they see someone levitate over a lake in broad daylight or instantly heal a condition that has resisted all treatment for years, the miracle can have a disempowering effect. The fact that someone else did what they hadn't been able to do themselves plays right into their subconscious beliefs of limitation.

When this happens, people tend to look to someone or something else to intervene where they feel powerless. They're looking for a savior, whether it's a drug or another person performing a miraculous healing. If we're convinced that we're powerless and dependent upon something beyond ourselves in order to have the experience, then we'll also feel the need to return to that "something" again and again to get what we need. We will, that is, until we realize that we can do for ourselves what is being done by someone else *for* us. It's at this point that the savior is no longer needed and we're truly healed.

### Experiencing Miracles from Afar:
### The Power of Mirror Neurons

Not everyone has the experience of being awed yet disempowered in the presence of a miracle. For some of us, witnessing one can have just the opposite effect—it can empower us by showing that a greater possibility exists. While the miracle itself may not be understood, what *is* clear is that another human has just done something that we thought was impossible. And when we see someone else do it, then we feel that we can do it as well. A new discovery about how the brain works may help us understand why we respond in this way.

In the late 1990s, a group of Italian neuroscientists discovered that a portion of the mammalian brain houses the memory of what they called "vocabularies of motor actions."[6] In other words, this special part of the brain, referred to as the *premotor cortex,* stores the rules for the way we act and respond in a given situation.

The key here is that the rules appear to be based on what we've already experienced. This discovery makes tremendous sense to me, having studied martial arts in my 20s and 30s. My instructors always began teaching a new movement by advising us to first "see" it in our minds again and again until it was natural and became second nature. When we use our imagination in this way and create in our minds what we're about to do in the world, these studies suggest that we're actually building the network of neural connections that make our live actions possible.

The researchers coined a new term for the special group of neurons that forms each of our libraries of possibilities. These cells are called *mirror neurons*. While the first studies were done with monkeys, new research shows that humans have what is described as an even "more elaborate" system of mirror neurons.[7] And it appears that they're activated in two different yet related types of circumstances:

1.   First, they become active when we perform a particular action, such as walking on a balance beam.

2.   Second, *our* mirror neurons become active when we watch *someone else* doing something that excites us. In other words, these cells appear to give us the ability to make what we see in others real within *us*.

This discovery has become the foundation for new research and a host of scientific papers exploring why fans can become so excited when watching their favorite sports heroes. We may be sitting on the couch with a plate of nachos and our favorite drink watching a wrestler on a Sunday afternoon, and while that competitor is embroiled in battle, *our* pulse will race, *our* breath will quicken, and *our* muscles will tighten, as if we were the ones on that mat.

This may sound like a silly example (especially if you're not into wrestling), but mirror neurons are also being studied in an effort to understand why a few violent fans at a soccer match can begin a scuffle that spreads until the situation becomes a full-blown riot. It all points back to the way we respond when we see someone else doing something with which we identify or to which we aspire. This is what makes mirror neurons so powerful in our discussion of miracles.

If we're the kind of person who simply needs a little boost in our confidence to prove that we can do what we've never done before, a miracle can go a long way. This may be precisely why the true teachers, healers, and miracle makers of history used the amazing feats of their day as they did. Both Jesus and Buddha enacted miracles to empower those who witnessed them. And both described these marvels as natural abilities that anyone could accomplish by learning what they had.

Buddha, for example, demonstrated everything from levitation, bilocation, and passing his hand through solid rock (as Milarepa did), to reading the minds of others to know their true beliefs, including their deepest fears. According to legend, in simply moving his hands over a ripe mango seed, he caused it to mature in compressed time and grow to a height of "50 hands" in a matter of only moments. Interestingly, however, he never considered what he did to be a miracle. To Buddha, these were the abilities that could be ours as the reward of knowing ourselves through deep meditation.

We've all heard of the miracles that Jesus performed in his life. For many, they've had the effect of making us feel "less than" the master who lived two millennia ago. While it sometimes comes to us in a lighthearted way, the impact of Jesus's role in our society and in our beliefs is enormous.

How many times have you told others that you were going to do something they believed wasn't feasible and they responded to your lofty goals by saying something like: "Oh yeah? Who do you think you are—Jesus Christ?" or "How are you going to get there—walk on water?" At such times, while we may laugh in the moment, what we've just experienced is an unconscious expression of a shared belief that Jesus did things we can't. If we're to believe his teachings and others, such as those of Buddha, however, nothing could be further from the truth.

In effect, Buddha asserted that his miracles were only extraordinary until we know ourselves and understand how the universe works. In words that may be more familiar in our culture, Jesus said the same thing. In response to the questions that his followers asked regarding his supernatural-appearing feats, he affirmed: "He who believes in me shall do the works which I do; and even greater than these things he shall do . . ."[8]

In language that is just as accurate today as it was 2,000 years ago, the great master is telling us of the power of mirror neurons. The studies have shown that these important receptors in the body do more than just respond to what they're exposed to. In the words of science writer Jonah Lehrer, they are "plastic, eager to modify their cortical networks in response to our viewing habits."[9]

In watching our favorite guitar player, sports hero, or artist, we actually can become better at what we do by being in their presence (live or recorded). Because we interpret what they do as real in our imagination, our mirror neurons help us to mimic and imitate what we've experienced. This is why a miracle can be so powerful in our lives. Not only does it blow the doors off of the limits that we may have held in place only moments before, witnessing it from an empowered perspective can give us what we need to achieve the same types of things in our own lives.

### A Small Miracle of Insight

Sometimes just when we need the power of miracles to change our beliefs, they materialize in the places we'd least expect. They can come to us as a drastic alteration in our physical reality or as a simple synchronicity in our lives. Sometimes they're big and can't be missed—the vision of Our Lady of the Rosary that appeared to 50,000 people on a hillside near Fátima, Portugal, in 1917, for example. Other times they're so subtle that if we aren't aware, we may miss them altogether. They can come from the lips of a stranger we suddenly and mysteriously encounter at just the right instant. If we listen carefully, we'll always hear the right words, at the right time, to dazzle us into a realization of something that we may have failed to notice only moments before.

※

On a cold January afternoon in 1989, I was hiking up the trail that leads to the top of Egypt's Mt. Horeb (the mountain of Moses). I'd spent the day in St. Catherine's Monastery and wanted to get to the peak by sunset to see the valley below. As I was winding up the narrow path, I'd occasionally see other hikers who were coming down from a day on the mountain. While they would generally pass with simply a nod or a greeting in another language, there was one man that day who did neither.

I saw him coming from the last switchback on the trail that led to the backside of the mountain. As he got closer, I could see that he was dressed differently from the other hikers I'd seen. Rather than the high-tech fabrics and styles that had been the norm, this man was wearing traditional Egyptian clothing. He wore a tattered, rust-colored galabia and obviously old and thick-soled sandals that were covered in dust. What made his appearance so odd, though, was that the man didn't even appear to be Egyptian! He was a small-framed Asian man, had very little hair, and was wearing round, wire-rimmed glasses.

As we neared one another, I was the first to speak. "Hello," I said, stopping on the trail for a moment to catch my breath. Not a sound came from the man as he walked closer. I thought that maybe he hadn't heard me or the wind had carried my voice away from him in another direction. Suddenly he stopped directly in front of me on the high side of the trail, looked up from the ground, and spoke a single sentence to me in English: "Sometimes you don't know what you have until you've lost it." As I took in what I had just heard, he simply stepped around me and continued his descent down the trail.

That moment in my life was a small miracle. The reason is less about what the man said and more about the timing and the context. The year was 1989, and the Cold War was drawing to a close. What the man on the trail couldn't have known is that it was during my Egyptian pilgrimage, and specifically during my hike to the top of Moses's mountain, that I'd set the time aside to make decisions that would affect my career in the defense industry, my friends, my family, and, ultimately, my life.

I had to ask myself what the chances were of an Asian man dressed in an Egyptian galabia coming down from the top of this historic mountain just when I was walking up, stopping before me, and offering his wisdom, seemingly from out of nowhere. My answer to my own question was easy: The odds were slim to none! In an encounter that lasted less than two minutes on a mountain halfway around the world from my home, a total stranger had brought clarity, and the hint of a warning, regarding the huge changes that I would make within a matter of days. In my way of thinking, that's a miracle.

I suspect that we all experience small miracles in our lives every day. Sometimes we have the wisdom and the courage to recognize them for what they are. In the moments when we don't, that's okay as well. It seems that our miracles have a way of coming back to us again and again. And each time they do, they become a little less subtle, until we can't possibly miss the message that they bring to our lives!

The key is that they're everywhere and occur every day for different reasons, in response to the different needs that we may have in the moment. Our job may be less about questioning the extraordinary things that happen in our daily lives and more about accepting the gifts they bring.

> **Try this:** When you go into the world today, before you leave your home, promise yourself that you'll find at least one miracle. Without any limits or bounds on what you think it should look like, simply state for yourself your clear intention that of the many miracles that cross your path, you'll recognize one of them. Then observe your world closely. The definition of the word *miracle* that I want you to use is "an event that appears inexplicable by the laws of nature." Once you choose to recognize them and accept them in your life, don't be surprised if they suddenly show up everywhere!

### Believing Our Way to a Greater Possibility

The last chapters have shown that when we ask ourselves to transcend our limitations, what we're really asking is to change our beliefs.

And to do so, we need a good reason. The corollary of this principle is that when the paradigm of an old belief is shattered, it must be done in the presence of others to have a widespread effect.

In all probability, some runner somewhere in the world could have run the four-minute mile a month before Roger Bannister ever did. And if he or she did so in the privacy of his or her own backyard track, where the only ones watching were the family pets, how could it be accepted by others? Like the sound of a tree that falls in the forest with no one to hear, who would ever know? Clearly our personal triumphs must be experienced by others to anchor them as a possibility in those people's lives. Each time we encounter a miracle, we upgrade *their* programs of belief and send consciousness a new blueprint for reality.

We've seen this principle at work many times. From Buddha, Jesus, and Mohammed to Gandhi, Mother Teresa, and Martin Luther King, Jr., each person lived a new way of being in the presence of others. They did so within the very consciousness that they chose to change. We may have heard about such powerful examples of transformation for so long that we take them for granted today. But a closer look at how these masters have seeded new ideas in an existing paradigm is nothing short of astonishing.

What makes their accomplishments so powerful is the way they implemented their changes. It's easy for a programmer to sit in an office somewhere with a bird's-eye view of a virtual computer world and see where changes need to be made. Once they're identified, the programmer can isolate portions of the program and modify them slightly or rewrite them altogether time and again until the output is just right.

The key here is that the programmer is outside the program looking in from a perspective where it's easy to see what's needed. So, in a sense, programmers are like Monday-morning quarterbacks reflecting back on a game that has already been played, where it's apparent in hindsight what should have happened. They're watching the game from the sidelines! And here is the reason why this makes what you and I do so much more powerful.

In our quantum consciousness computer, we're *not* on the sidelines. We're in the same program that we're trying to change! We're searching for meaning, healing, peace, and abundance within the very program where we've experienced the lack of those things. In computer-science lingo, when a program has the capacity to evaluate an ever-changing situation and come up with a new response, it's said to have intelligence. Because the intelligence is machine generated, it's said to be artificial.

A recent example of artificial intelligence that made worldwide headlines is the computer named Deep Blue.[10] Designed specifically as a chess-playing program, Deep Blue won Game 1 against the reigning world champion, Garry Kasparov, in a February 10, 1996, match that was seen around the world. Afterward, Kasparov commented that the computer program showed "deep intelligence" and "creativity" that even the chess master couldn't understand.

In some respects, we may not be so different from Deep Blue. Within the consciousness computer of the universe, we're evaluating the conditions that life throws our way and making the best choices possible using the information that we have. The key here is that we tend to come to those decisions based on what we *believe* about our capabilities and limits within the universe. As we recognize that everyday reality is the palette that displays our possibilities, rather than being the reflection of our limitations, what we may have considered inconceivable in the past now is within our grasp. Suddenly everything that we could ever imagine, and probably things that we've never even considered, become possible within this way of thinking.

In the beginning of this book, I used the patterns of sound in water as an analogy for the way our "belief waves" ripple through the quantum stuff of which the universe is made. Without describing exactly how the ripples move, the idea was that the experience we call "belief" has an effect that extends well beyond our bodies where it's created. In that effect we find our power.

As we learn to hone the quality of our beliefs in very precise ways, we're learning to change the belief waves of disease into healing, the patterns of war into peace, and failure and lack into success and abundance in our world. What could be more powerful? What could be more sacred? Is it any wonder that everything from religions to nations have been built around the power of our beliefs?

# A Users' Guide to the Universe

*"Your whole life can change in a second, and*
*you never even know when it's coming."*
— from the movie *Before and After,* as quoted
by Laurence Galian in *The Sun At Midnight:*
*The Revealed Mysteries of the Ahlul Bayt Sufis*

*"Every human being is the author of his own health or disease."*
— **Buddha** (c. 563 B.C.E.–c. 483 B.C.E.)

Years ago, I remember seeing a *Star Trek: The Next Generation* episode that changed everything I believed about virtual reality. The story line begins with the crew of the *Enterprise* exploring an uncharted area of deep space. In this particular episode, they make the surprising discovery that a distant sun is about to explode into a supernova. What makes this event so significant is that it's happening in a solar system with an Earth-like planet that supports human life—people who are certain to be destroyed within a few short hours by the exploding sun.

The problem comes from the desire of the *Enterprise*'s crew to save the humans, which opposes their prime directive to avoid disturbing the development of any less-advanced civilizations at all costs. If the captain and his team were suddenly to "beam" down to the planet for a rescue mission, they would certainly be perceived as gods in the developing civilization, and those perceptions would forever change the course of its history. But not to worry! To save the inhabitants without shocking them into a new religion, the crew comes up with a brilliant plan.

Using their teleportation and virtual-reality capabilities (both of which are actually in various stages of development today), they decide to wait until night comes and the inhabitants of the planet are asleep. Then they will carefully teleport the entire population into a simulation on the *Enterprise* designed to mimic their reality—a *virtual* reality. Having done so, they will then fly them to a new home in another solar system that looks, feels, and works just like their soon-to-be-destroyed planet. When the people wake up from their sleep, they'll never know what's happened. They won't know that they're hurtling through space at a gazillion miles per hour in the virtual reality of a simulated world. And if they should suspect that anything has happened, it will just seem like a dream. To them, everything will appear to be business as usual. They'll soon find themselves in a safe, familiar world and never know any differently.

Even the best-laid plans can go awry, however, and the events in this particular episode are no exception. At first, everything appears to be great. While asleep, the inhabitants are teleported into their virtual reality. When they wake up, they accept their location as the real deal—they do, that is, until the power systems for the starship fail and can no longer hold the computer simulation in place. Suddenly, the virtual reality begins to fall apart: The rocks flicker, fade, and become transparent; the heavens change from blue sky to the dome of the starship's holodeck; and the technicians who have been invisible to those in the simulation suddenly come into view. Needless to say, the entire plot changes; and the well-intentioned rescue becomes an exercise in sensitivity, truth, and human emotion.

My point is simply this: The inhabitants of the planet didn't know they were in a virtual reality until it began to fail. That's the whole idea of a simulation—it's *supposed* to be so real that we can use it to master our skills as pilots, athletes, or creators just as if it were the real thing. So, if we were in a virtual simulation designed to mimic a higher dimension, or heaven, here on Earth, would we ever even know it?

*Is Life Real, or Is It a Dream?*
*Can We Tell the Difference?*

When something is true, it's not unusual to find that the truth shows up in a number of different places and in varying ways. Our experience of beauty in others is a perfect example. When we encounter people who appeal to us as truly beautiful, inside and out, their beauty is timeless and enduring. Because we see them through our perception of attractiveness, no matter how closely we examine their lives, they remain beautiful to us. They are beautiful when they wake up, when they do their work, when they make mistakes, and at the end of their day. Clarifying this phenomenon, the Elizabethan poet Fulke Greville stated, "The criterion of true beauty is that it increases on examination."[1]

In the same way that Greville believed that beauty holds up under close scrutiny, we'd expect that the theme underlying a universal truth would remain consistent the more we explore it. The biblical Flood offers a perfect example of just such a theme. Throughout history and cultures, the story of a vast flood is recounted around the world. Playing out on various continents, in different languages, and involving diverse people, the details and the outcome are nearly identical. It's this consistent theme—and the evidence that supports it—that leads us to believe that at some point in our distant past a great flood actually occurred.

Similar to the way the flood account appears in many traditions, the birth of the universe and the story of our origins is recounted with remarkable consistency across different worldviews. The bottom line that weaves such narratives together is the description of our world as a dream/illusion/projection of things happening in another realm.

And now we must consider the new evidence of Earth as a simulation among those views.

When we think about such a possibility, it's not really so different from the ideas that form the basis for nearly every major spiritual tradition today. From the Hindu cosmology that describes the universe as a dream of Vishnu to the people of the Kalahari of southern Africa who say that we're dreaming our own existence, spiritual traditions portray our reality as being the shadow of another—a reality that's even more real than this one. What's interesting here is that the theme of the stories doesn't change. Regardless of when they began, the idea of this being an illusory world is a constant, even in the oldest accounts of creation.

Australia's Aboriginal inhabitants, for example, can be traced back through a continuous bloodline that began at least 50,000 years ago, and possibly before. Throughout that vast period of time, their creation story has been preserved. In much the same way that new theories suggest that an ancient programmer fashioned our world, the Aborigines describe the *Wondjinas,* the ancestral beings that created this world by dreaming it into existence. What's important here is that each of these traditions describes our connection to another realm beyond what we can perceive from our vantage point here on Earth.

During his lifetime, the pioneering physicist David Bohm offered a similar worldview in modern language. Through terms such as the *implicate order* and the *explicate order,* Bohm saw our world as the shadow or the projection of events that are happening somewhere else.[2] He viewed that somewhere as a deeper reality from which the events of our world emerge. Similar to the teachings of indigenous traditions, Bohm's work demonstrated that this other realm is very real, perhaps even more so than *ours.* Again, it's just that we can't see it from where we are now.

Except for their language, these perspectives parallel what the great religions have said for centuries. The theme that they share is that we're living in a temporary world where we're testing, training, and preparing ourselves for something that's yet to come, in a realm that we've yet to see. While the stories of precisely what that something is and how we get there may vary among traditions, all seem to deal with the power of belief and our ability to believe our hearts' desires into existence.

From this perspective, when we find ourselves in situations that challenge and test us, we're actually honing our skills of belief for use in a place that's identified by names that range from Nirvana and the fifth world to higher dimensions and heaven. In the event that we fail to master those forces here, we're given an additional opportunity, under even more intense conditions, in another dream, which the Christian traditions simply call hell. It's from these age-old beliefs that the idea of life as a simulation gets really interesting.

### If We Were Living in a Simulation, Would We Know It?

When, as a scientist, I began to consider our world as a simulation and belief as the language of mastery, the first question that came to mind was: *Why?* What would be the purpose? What end could possibly justify the effort required to create an artificial reality the size of the whole universe? The first thing I did was to look up the terms *simulation* and *virtual reality* to know what they really mean. Through their definitions, I found myself one step closer to answering my initial question.

*The American Heritage College Dictionary* defines *virtual reality* as "a computer simulation of a real or imaginary system that enables a user to perform operations on the simulated system and show the effects in real time."[3] In other words, it's an artificial environment of action and feedback, where we can discover the effects of our behavior and the consequences of our conduct in "safe" surroundings. While this definition is interesting, when we combine it with the description of a simulation, it offers a modern context for some of the most mysterious religious traditions of the past—especially those describing our miraculous possibilities.

The same dictionary's definition of a *simulation* is brief yet powerful: "the imitation or representation of a potential situation."[4] Doesn't this sound eerily similar to what our experience of Earth is in relation to heaven? When we put these two definitions together and consider them within the context of our deepest beliefs and most cherished spiritual traditions, the implications are dizzying. They describe precisely the same things that we've been told by millennia-old texts—specifically, that we're living in the temporary "representation of a potential situation" (heaven or a higher dimension) that allows us to learn the rules here before we get to the real thing.

Maybe that's the best way to think of what's happening in our world today. We're being given greater opportunities, under more extreme conditions, with more powerful consequences so that we can find out which of our beliefs work and which ones don't. The intensity with which the opportunities seem to be coming our way suggests that it's important that we learn these lessons soon, before we find ourselves in a place where such skills are a must.

In recent years, I've shared this possibility with live audiences all over the world. The response has been overwhelmingly, almost unanimously, positive. Perhaps it's because our high-tech world has already prepared us for such an idea. Maybe it's because Max Planck's description of the matrix and the movie based on his ideas have already planted the seed for the existence of a greater reality. For whatever reason, almost universally, audience participants not only accept that such a possibility exists, but also feel as though they've been getting ready for something like this throughout their lives.

When I think about why some people might be so willing to accept what sounds to others like such a radical idea, two possibilities come to mind:

1. We may simply be ready for a new story of our existence—or at least an updated version of the existing one—that tells us who we are and how the universe began.

2. The idea of our living in a state of virtual reality rings so true and touches something so deep within us that we've been waiting for the right words to trigger just such a possibility in our memory.

When we look at the parallels between a virtual simulation and a religious description of life, the connection is unmistakable. Following is a high-level summary comparing the two views of reality.

| Comparison Between Virtual Reality and Spiritual Reality | |
|---|---|
| **Virtual Reality** | **Spiritual Reality** |
| 1. Created by a programmer | 1. Created by a Higher Power/ God |
| 2. Has a start and a stop | 2. Has the beginning and the end of time |
| 3. Rules/user improves with practice | 3. Lessons repeated until mastered |
| 4. User is connected "outside" of simulation | 4. We are connected to higher self/source/God |
| 5. User has entry and exit points | 5. We experience birth and death |
| 6. User defines experience from within | 6. Reality mirrors our experience |

The similarities are striking. Except for the language, these two ways of thinking of the world sound nearly identical.

### *"We Almost Certainly Live in a Simulation":*
### *The Evidence*

In 2002, Oxford University's Nick Bostrom, a leading philosopher and the director of the Future of Humanity Institute, carried the radical idea of our living in a virtual reality one step further. In bold language, he explored it through a no-nonsense paper entitled "Are You Living in a Computer Simulation?" in which he applies the rigors of mathematics and logic to give us a concrete way to consider, somehow or another, whether or not "reality" is real.[5]

He begins by describing the possibility of a future civilization that has survived the threats of war, disease, and natural disasters to become what he calls "posthuman." He then identifies three scenarios through a complex statistical analysis (omitted here for simplicity) and argues that at least one of them is true. The possibilities are as follows:

1. Some catastrophic event (such as a global war, natural disaster, widespread disease, and so on) will destroy us before we ever reach the posthuman stage.

2. We reach the posthuman stage but have little interest in creating universe-sized simulations of reality.

3. We reach the posthuman stage, we have the interest and/or the need to create a virtual world, and we actually do so.

In a section of the paper that describes what he calls "the core of the simulation argument," Bostrom asks a fundamental question: *If there were a substantial chance that our civilization would ever get to the posthuman stage and run what he calls "ancestor-simulations," then how come we're not living such a simulation now?*

Based on the current trends of science, Bostrom logically assumes that a technologically mature posthuman civilization would include enormous computing power.[6] With this "empirical fact" in mind, his statistics show that at least one of his three propositions must be true.

If the first or second is true, then the probability that we're living in a simulation is slim. The third possibility is where things get really interesting—if *it* is true, he concludes, "*we almost certainly live in a simulation* [my emphasis]."[7] In other words, if it's likely that our species survives the things that threaten our future and has the interest or need to create a simulated world, then the technology that comes under such conditions will allow us to do so. This leads to the conclusion that the odds favor the idea that these things have already happened and that we're already living in a simulated universe.

Regardless of how we may feel about such a conclusion or how mind-boggling it may appear, what I believe is important here is that the whole idea of our living in a virtual reality be taken so seriously that it's given the time and energy required to explore it as a very real solution to the mystery of our existence.

> The evidence suggests that we almost certainly live in a virtual reality.

Recognizing that we have the power to destroy ourselves—as the first possibility in Bostrom's paper describes, yet coming from a very different perspective on the topic—British astrophysicist Stephen Hawking suggests that we'll need to find another world to inhabit if the human species is to survive. During a 2006 press conference in Hong Kong, he stated: "We won't find anywhere as nice as Earth unless we go to another star system."[8]

While I certainly understand the thinking behind Hawking's view, and ultimately believe that human beings *will* be living on other worlds, I also feel that to develop the technology to do so, we'll have to answer the question posed in this book: *What is the role of belief in our world?* It may well be that when we discover how the universe and belief really work, we'll find less need to make another planet our home. As we master our power of belief, Earth will change as a result of our lessons and reflect our desire to live sustainable, cooperative, and peaceful lives.

When we combine the evidence suggesting that we're already living in a state of virtual reality with the wisdom of indigenous traditions, which tell us that the universe is a dream that mirrors our beliefs, suddenly the whole idea of our power to change the world becomes more plausible. It's worth exploring the evidence that belief *itself* is the language that brings joy or suffering to our lives—and with a new urgency!

All of this leads to even deeper questions. *Who* could be responsible for the virtual experience of an entire universe? Who put this all together, and who wrote the code? While the movies like to answer such questions through the existence of a mysterious "architect" lurking behind the scenes, we may find that it's actually something much simpler . . . yet even more profound.

### Did the Great Programmer Leave Us a Manual?

Early in the movie *Contact,* the main character, Dr. Arroway (played by Jodie Foster), is part of a research team that receive an encrypted message from deep space. Before they can decode it, the team must find a key that tells them that their translations are correct. Rather than a hidden key buried in a text or complex mathematical formula, this code is found in a place where its programmers were certain that it would remain safe: It's in the message itself. By translating a simple phrase within it, Dr. Arroway's team unlocks the secret of Earth's first interstellar calling card.

Maybe the same principle applies to uncovering the secret of how our beliefs work in a simulated reality. The clue as to "who" is responsible may lie in identifying who it is that benefits from such an experience. Who is better off by mastering the rules of such a practice world? The answer is obvious yet mysterious. It's those in the simulation itself. It's *us!*

We may just discover that *we're the great programmers* who have created this practice world for ourselves. We may find that *we've agreed* to immerse ourselves in the feedback loop of a simulation to master our hearts. What better way to learn how to live in a realm that we've yet to inhabit?

If this is the case, then it makes even more sense to look within the mystery of what we've created to find the rules of our creation. As mentioned earlier, whether we believe that we're actually in such a simulated place or merely use it as a metaphor for what we experience in life makes little difference. What's important is that, real or virtual, we're here now. And the rules of "here" are what we're learning to master.

Jürgen Schmidhuber of Switzerland's Dalle Molle Institute for Artificial Intelligence is one of the leading proponents of the idea that our world is the result of a great cosmic computer. Lacking only the words that say, *"In a galaxy far, far, away . . ."* Schmidhuber leaves little doubt as to how he believes our universe began, stating, "A long time ago, the Great Programmer wrote a program that runs all possible universes on His Big Computer."[9] In his paper entitled "A Computer Scientist's View of Life, the Universe, and Everything," he offers a technical yet compelling argument, similar to Bostrom's analysis, proposing that it's more likely that we *are* living in a virtual reality than not.

So what do these analyses mean? If we're here in a world of infinite possibilities to master what it means to be in such a place, did anyone leave us the instructions? Did Schmidhuber's Great Programmer leave us a users' manual? If so, would we recognize it if we found it?

For the last 300 years or so, we've relied upon the "laws" of physics to tell us the rules of our world: both what's possible and what's not. For the most part, those laws seem to have worked well . . . at least they do so in the everyday world. As mentioned before, however, there are places where the laws of physics don't operate, such as the very small realm of quantum particles. While it would seem that this world plays such an insignificant role in our lives that we could just write off the failure of physical laws as a fringe effect, nothing could be further from the truth. The very place where the laws break down is precisely where our reality begins.

The fact that the laws of physics as we know them today don't appear to be universal tells us that there must be other rules that govern our reality. If we can find them and learn what they mean in our lives, then the instructions for what's possible and what's not will become clear. This is where the power of belief comes in. Because belief is considered to be among the effects that aren't accounted for by conventional physics, they may just point the way to understanding how our simulation works.

In Chapter 1, I shared the story of my experience at the Taos Pueblo. When someone asked our Native American guide about his "secret" healing traditions, he answered that the best way to hide something is "to keep it in plain sight." His comment is reminiscent of the way the code to Dr. Arroway's message was located in plain sight in the message itself, and leads us to the question: *Has something similar happened to us?* Is our users' manual to reality being presented to us in a form that's so abundant that while looking for subtle clues, we've missed it altogether? . . . I believe the answer is *yes*.

The users' manual to reality is reality itself. What better way to show how a reflected universe works than to have the instant feedback of relationships, abundance, health, and joy—or the lack of all these things—so that we can see what works and what doesn't? We can try *this* way of being (or *that* way of being), and if we have the wisdom to recognize how our world changes when we modify our beliefs, we have our paperless users' guide as a lifetime of experience. It all comes down to patterns of energy, how they interact, and how we affect them with our beliefs.

### Prayer as a Program

In the previous chapters we've explored the discoveries and traditions reminding us that belief, as well as the way we feel about it, is the language that makes things happen in the world. The beauty of belief is that we don't have to understand it to benefit from it in our lives. And this is the message of the masters from our past.

In the words of their time, teachers such as Buddha, Jesus, Krishna, Native American elders, and others did their best to share the secret that frees us from being victims of life. In a very real sense, they were the master programmers of consciousness as well as the architects of the ages. And they didn't try to keep the secret of rearranging atoms to make miracles to themselves—they taught us the code to do the same things and become programmers of reality, too. We've inherited their teachings. As mystical as their words may seem to us today, can you imagine how they would have sounded to a largely illiterate population 2,500 years ago?

Buddha, for example, was a man far ahead of his time. When he was asked to explain our role in the events that happen in the world, his answer was clear, concise, and deep: "All things appear and disappear because of the concurrence of causes and conditions."[10] He also said, "Nothing ever exists entirely alone; everything is in relation to everything else."[11] What powerful and eloquent words! What could they have possibly meant to the people of his time? Once he discovered this truth for himself, Buddha spent the rest of his life teaching students how we can change the world by changing ourselves.

In a similar manner, Jesus taught that we must *become* in life the very things that we choose to experience in the world. Searching for a way to demonstrate that our quantum reality will mirror what we give it to work with, he admonished his followers not to be swayed by the anger and injustice of those around them. Rather, he demonstrated that our beliefs have the power to change us, and when we change ourselves, we change our world.

To experience such powerful beliefs, the masters of times past chose just the right words, designed to elicit just the right feelings, in order to create just the right effects. Today we call their belief programs "prayers," and we can think of them as instructions to consciousness. When we speak the words of the code, they're designed to create the heart-based beliefs of healing and miracles. The Lord's Prayer is a beautiful example.

As we examine this powerful prayer as a code, we notice that the words fall into the precise framework of the computer programs described in Chapter 2. In what may well be the oldest and most widely documented description of such a program, Jesus left us a template explaining how we may speak to the quantum essence of the universe, and how to do so in a way that it recognizes. In a language that is as clear and elegant today as it was 2,000 years ago, Jesus begins his programming instructions by stating simply and directly how the code is to be used: *"After this manner therefore pray ye."* The language is important here. Clearly he didn't say only to pray using these *exact* words. Rather, he invited us to pray *like this,* or in this way, or "after this manner." We have options.

Following his admonition, he stated the words of the program designed to communicate our hearts' desires to the universe. Although the Lord's Prayer may already be familiar to you, let's examine it through the eyes of a cosmic programmer. When we do, it clearly falls into our three familiar categories of the *begin, work,* and *completion* commands.

| The Code | Program Command | Purpose |
|---|---|---|
| *The Lord's Prayer* <br> Our Father who art in heaven, <br> Hallowed be thy name. <br> Thy kingdom come, <br> Thy will be done on earth, <br> as it is in heaven. | *Begin* command | Opens the field |

This group of statements clearly marks the start, or the *beginning*, of our consciousness code. They aren't asking us to do anything or be anything—they're statements of adoration, acknowledging the power of the force that we're about to access. When we read them from the perspective of prayer as a code, they're designed to inspire in us a sense of openness and greatness. It is this welling up of feeling that opens the path of possibility from our hearts into the quantum field. And the begin command clearly leaves us with a very different feeling from the words in the next part of the code.

| The Code | Program Command | Purpose |
|---|---|---|
| Give us this day our daily bread, <br> And forgive us our debts, <br> as we forgive our debtors. <br> And lead us not into temptation, <br> but deliver us from evil. | *Work* command | Creates the feeling |

These statements are the work commands. Rather than inspiring us with the feeling that we're about to commune with the universe itself, they provide the action for the prayer to accomplish. In this instance, that action is the feeling that comes from being relieved of the burdens identified in the prayer. When we believe that we have everything we need for our families, and ourselves, we experience a sense of relief. When we sense that we're free of the tension between us and those to whom we're beholden, then we feel that we're being led on the right path and we're enveloped in a healing sense of peace and gratitude. This is the work that the program is designed to accomplish.

| The Code | Program Command | Purpose |
|---|---|---|
| For thine is the kingdom, and the power, and the glory, for ever. Amen. | *Completion* command | Closure of thanks |

With the completion-command statements, once again there is a definite shift in tone and sense. They're no longer telling our program what to do; instead, they're designed to provide a sense of closure. When we say them, we feel that completion as a release in our body. Our prayer isn't left lingering as an open-ended proposition; rather, it has an ending. It's clean, clear, and complete. When we declare that the universe is in the hands of a greater power and we feel that we're aligned with that power to bring our words to life, we find a sense of empowerment. After using this template, we know that our prayer has been accomplished.

The beauty of the Lord's Prayer is its tradition and its simplicity. Through a blueprint that has changed little in more than 2,000 years, we're given the structure for a cosmic code to open the field of infinite possibilities. Just as the code of a computer program links us with the unseen mechanisms that allow the machine to do what it does, the words of this prayer are designed to manifest the conditions that link us with the forces of creation. Within the words of the prayer we find the great secret to programming the universe, and it's hidden in plain sight!

> **Try this:** Look at the great prayers of other traditions.
> See for yourself if and how their authors have used the
> template of *begin, work,* and *completion* commands that
> we see in the Lord's Prayer to speak to the universe.

### A Users' Guide to the Universe

In the last chapter of *The Divine Matrix,* I listed the book's high-lights as a series of keys that summarize the principles described throughout its pages. Because this book dovetails with that material, I've done something similar here, listing the belief codes that have been highlighted in each chapter.

In the first six chapters, these ideas were developed in a precise sequence—they have an order, and there's a reason for it. Every one is offered within the context of the ideas that precede it, while paving the way for those that follow. Similar to *The Divine Matrix*'s keys, I invite you to consider the following sequence of belief codes one at a time. Allow each its own merit as a powerful agent of change.

In his book *The Prophet,* Kahlil Gibran reminds us: "Work is love made visible."[12] From this perspective, it's through your actions that you show your caring for life itself, so I invite you to *work* with your belief codes. Allow them to become your love made visible. Read each one and ponder it, discuss it, share it, and live with it until it makes sense to you. Together, these steps can become your consciousness program for changing yourself and your world.

**Belief Code 1:** Experiments show that the focus of our attention changes reality itself and suggest that we live in an interactive universe.

**Belief Code 2:** We live our lives based on what we believe about our world, ourselves, our capabilities, and our limits.

**Belief Code 3:** Science is a language—one of many that describe us, the universe, our bodies, and how things work.

**Belief Code 4:** If the particles that we're made of can be in instantaneous communication with one another, be in two places at once, and even change the past through choices made in the present, then we can as well.

**Belief Code 5:** Our beliefs have the power to change the flow of events in the universe—literally to interrupt and redirect time, matter, and space, and the events that occur within them.

**Belief Code 6:** Just as we can run a simulated program that looks and feels real, studies suggest that the universe itself may be the output of a huge and ancient simulation—a computer program—that began long ago. If so, then to know the program's code is to know the rules of reality itself.

**Belief Code 7:** When we think of the universe as a program, atoms represent "bits" of information that work just the way familiar computer bits do. They are either "on," as physical matter, or "off," as invisible waves.

**Belief Code 8:** Nature uses a few simple, self-similar, and repeating patterns—fractals—to build atoms into the familiar patterns of everything from elements and molecules to rocks, trees, and us.

**Belief Code 9:** If the universe is made of repeating patterns, then to understand something on a small scale provides a powerful window into similar forms on a grand scale.

**Belief Code 10:** Belief is the "program" that creates patterns in reality.

**Belief Code 11:** What we *believe* to be true in life may be more powerful than what others accept as truth.

**Belief Code 12:** We must accept the power of belief to tap it in our lives.

**Belief Code 13:** Belief is defined as the certainty that comes from accepting what we *think is true* in our minds, coupled with what we *feel is true* in our hearts.

**Belief Code 14:** Belief is expressed in the heart, where our experiences are translated into the electrical and magnetic waves that interact with the physical world.

**Belief Code 15:** Beliefs, and the feelings that we have about them, are the language that "speaks" to the quantum stuff that makes our reality.

**Belief Code 16:** The subconscious mind is larger and faster than the conscious mind, and can account for as much as 90 percent of our activity each day.

**Belief Code 17:** Many of our most deeply held beliefs are subconscious and begin when our brain state allows us to absorb the ideas of others before the age of seven.

**Belief Code 18:** In our greatest challenges of life we often find that our deeply hidden beliefs are exposed and available for healing.

**Belief Code 19:**  Our beliefs about unresolved hurt can create physical effects with the power to damage or even kill us.

**Belief Code 20:**  When our soul hurts, our pain is transmitted into the body as the spiritual quality of the life force that we feed into each cell.

**Belief Code 21:**  The same principles that allow us to hurt ourselves into death also work in reverse, allowing us to heal ourselves into life.

**Belief Code 22:**  Our belief in one force for everything that happens in the world, or two opposite and opposing forces—good and evil—plays out in our experience of life, health, relationships, and abundance.

**Belief Code 23:**  To heal the ancient battle between darkness and light, we may find that it's less about defeating one or the other, and more about choosing our relationship to both.

**Belief Code 24:**  A miracle that's possible for anyone is possible for everyone.

**Belief Code 25:**  In a participatory reality, we are creating our experience, as well as experiencing what we have created.

**Belief Code 26:**  In 1998, scientists confirmed that photons are influenced just by being "watched" and discovered that the more intense the watching, the greater the watcher's influence on how the particles behave.

**Belief Code 27:** The prime rule of reality is that we must *become* in our lives what we choose to experience in the world.

**Belief Code 28:** We tend to experience in life what we identify with in our beliefs.

**Belief Code 29:** For different reasons that reflect the variations in the way we learn, both logic and miracles give us a way into the deepest recesses of our beliefs.

**Belief Code 30:** To change our beliefs through the logic of our minds, we must convince ourselves of a new possibility through inarguable facts that lead to an inescapable conclusion.

**Belief Code 31:** The power of a miracle is that we don't have to understand *why* it works. We must, however, be willing to accept what it brings to our lives.

### The Spontaneous Healing of Belief

Almost universally, we share a sense that there's more to us than meets the eye. Somewhere deep inside, we *know* we have miraculous powers that we simply haven't tapped—at least not in this lifetime. We also know that we have the ability to bring the miracles of our imagination into the reality of our lives. Maybe it's *because* we're aware that these things are possible that we find the strength to love fearlessly and share unselfishly in a world that often looks dangerously out of control.

From the time we're children, we fantasize about our untapped powers. We imagine doing things that are beyond the realm of what other people say is possible—flying among the clouds, for instance, and talking to animals and beings that other people can't see. And why not? While we're still children, we haven't learned differently. As children, we haven't learned that things don't exist unless we can see them, and that miracles can't happen in our lives. In the clarity of what we believe, we see those things and recognize miracles all around us.

As we've described in this book, whether we're talking about the universe, the world, or our bodies, the miracles of life are ultimately the expressions of something that begins deep within us. They result from our truly astonishing ability to transform quantum energy into the stuff of reality. The transformation happens through the power of our beliefs. Nothing more and nothing less!

What would it mean to you if you could suddenly awaken your deepest passions and greatest aspirations and bring them to life? Wouldn't you like to find out? That's precisely what this book is all about.

It all begins with our power to free ourselves from the false limits of the past. Through the healing of our beliefs, we discover how—with the grace and ease that comes from experiencing ourselves as part of the world rather than separate from it. When we do so, we become the seed of life's miracles, as well as the miracles themselves.

In the pure space of our beliefs, where all things begin, we can see hideous diseases such as HIV disappear from our own bodies, just like the four-year-old boy who demonstrated precisely such a miracle in 1995 while under study at the UCLA School of Medicine.[13] We can also see ourselves transcend the limits of our past, as Amanda Dennison did in her record-breaking fire walk in 2005. Yet, even in the glimmer of such possibilities, we still need something real to remind us—something that tells us beyond any doubt that our miraculous potential is real, not just an idea that we're making up because we want it to be true.

Our everyday world is that something.

In life, we find the reminders of how we can share the power of our belief. Sometimes it can happen in a big way that can't be missed, and sometimes it occurs so subtly that only we will ever know. When we see other people, for example, as blossoming in their greatest strengths rather than shriveling in their occasional weakness, our beliefs become the seed for healing their perceptions. When we accept our own perfection instead of focusing on the inadequacies that others are quick to point out to us, we experience the same healing for ourselves.

Our job is to look into the world for reasons to believe in ourselves. Each time we find one, it replaces the limitations that we may have held ourselves to in the past. It's when we abandon ourselves to that new possibility that we shatter the old paradigm of false limits and find the spontaneous healing of our beliefs.

> *"Your work is to discover your world and then*
> *with all your heart give yourself to it."*
> — **Buddha**

# ACKNOWLEDGMENTS

*The Spontaneous Healing of Belief* is a synthesis of the research, discoveries, and presentations that began with a small living-room audience in Denver, Colorado, in 1986. While it's impossible to mention by name each person whose work is reflected in this book, I take this opportunity to express my deepest gratitude to the following:

Every one of the really great people at Hay House. I offer my sincere appreciation and many thanks to Louise Hay, Reid Tracy, and Ron Tillinghast, for your vision and dedication to the truly extraordinary way of doing business that has become the hallmark of Hay House's success. To Reid Tracy, president and CEO, once again I send my deepest gratitude for your faith in me and my work. To Jill Kramer, editorial director, many, many thanks for your honest opinions, for your guidance, for magically being at your phone every time I call, and for the years of experience that you bring to each of our conversations.

Courtney Pavone, my publicist; Alex Freemon, my copy editor; Jacqui Clark, publicity director; Jeannie Liberati, sales director; Margarete Nielson, marketing director; Nancy Levin, event director; Georgene Cevasco, audio publishing manager; and Rocky George, audio engineer extraordinaire—I could not ask for a nicer group of people to work with, or a more dedicated team to support my work. Your excitement and professionalism are unsurpassed. I'm proud to be a part of all the good things that the Hay House family brings to our world.

Ned Leavitt, my literary agent: Many thanks for the wisdom and integrity that you bring to each milestone we cross together. Through your guidance in shepherding our books through the publishing world, we have reached more people than ever before with our empowering message of hope and possibility. While I deeply appreciate your impeccable guidance, I am especially grateful for your trust and friendship.

Stephanie Gunning, many thanks for your patience, your clarity, and the dedication that's reflected in all that you do. Most of all, thank you for sharing the journey that helps me to hone my words while honoring the integrity of my message as my frontline editor extraordinaire.

Lauri Willmot, my favorite (and only) office manager: You have my continued admiration and countless thanks for your dedication, patience, and willingness to adapt to the changes in both of our lives. Many thanks for being there for nearly ten years, and especially when it counts!

Robin and Jerry Miner, everyone at Source Books, and all of the affiliates that have become our spiritual family—my deep gratitude and heartfelt thanks for staying with me over the years. I love you all.

To my mom, Sylvia, and my brother, Eric, thank you for your support even in the times you may not have understood me or agreed with my decisions. Through a lifetime of dramatic change that has not always been easy, we have remained a family: small, yet close. As our journey continues, I see with greater clarity the blessing that you are in my life, and with each day my appreciation for you grows while my love for you deepens.

To my dear friend Bruce Lipton, knowing you and Margaret and touring the world together has been an inspiration, an honor, and a blessing. My most sincere thanks for your brilliant mind, life-changing work, beautiful heart, and, most of all, the gift of your friendship.

To Jonathan Goldman, my brother in spirit and dear friend in life. Knowing that I can count on your wisdom, love, and support means more than I could ever express. My days are richer with you in them, and I count you and Andi among the great blessings in my life.

To the one person who sees me at my very best, and my very worst, Kennedy, my beloved wife and partner in life—thank you for your enduring love, unwavering support, brilliant mind, and your patience with our really long days, really short nights, and good mornings from the other side of the world. Most of all, thank you for the blessing of our journey together, for believing in me always, and for sharing just the right words that heal in ways that you could never know!

A very special thanks to everyone who has supported our work, books, recordings, and live presentations over the years. I am honored by your trust and in awe of your vision for a better world. Through your presence, I have learned to become a better listener and heard the words that allow me to share our empowering message of hope and possibility. To all, I remain grateful always.

❋  ❋  ❋

# ENDNOTES

· · · · · · · · · · · · · · · · · · · · · · · · · · · · · · · · · · · · · · · · ·

*Introduction*

1. Spoken by physicist John Archibald Wheeler and quoted in the online version of *Science & Spirit* in an article, "The Beauty of Truth" (2007). Website: **www.science-spirit.org/article_detail.php?article_id=308**.

2. Quote by physicist Albert Einstein in an article in *Discover*, "Einstein's Gift for Simplicity" (September 30, 2004). Website: **http://discovermagazine.com/2004/sep/einsteins-gift-for-simplicity/article_view?b_start:int=1&-C=**.

3. Gregg Braden, *The Divine Matrix: Bridging Time, Space, Miracles, and Belief* (Carlsbad, CA: Hay House, 2007): p. 54.

4. Malcolm W. Browne, "Signal Travels Farther and Faster Than Light," Thomas Jefferson National Accelerator Facility (Newport News, VA) online newsletter (July 22, 1997). Website: **www.cebaf.gov/news/internet/1997/spooky.html**.

5. This effect was first reported in Russia: P.P. Gariaev, K.V. Grigor'ev, A.A. Vasil'ev, V.P. Poponin, and V.A. Shcheglov, "Investigation of the Fluctuation Dynamics of DNA Solutions by Laser Correlation Spectroscopy," *Bulletin of the Lebedev Physics Institute*, nos. 11–12 (1992): pp. 23–30; as cited by Vladimir Poponin in an online article, "The DNA Phantom Effect: Direct Measurement of a New Field in the Vacuum Substructure," *Update on DNA Phantom Effect* (March 19, 2002). The Weather Master Website: **www.twm.co.nz/DNAPhantom.htm**.

6. Glen Rein and Rollin McCraty, "Structural Changes in Water and DNA Associated with New Physiologically Measurable States," *Journal of Scientific Exploration*, vol. 8, no. 3 (1994): pp. 438–439.

7. A beautiful example of applying what we know about inner peace to a wartime situation is found in the pioneering study done by David W. Orme-Johnson, Charles N. Alexander, John L. Davies, Howard M. Chandler, and Wallace E. Larimore, "International Peace Project in the Middle East," *The Journal of Conflict Resolution*, vol. 32, no. 4 (December 1988): p. 778.

8. A second example of applying what we know about the focused power of feeling and belief to the condition of a life-threatening condition comes from *101 Miracles of Natural Healing*, a step-by-step instructional video in the Chi-Lel™ method of healing created by founder Dr. Pang Ming. Website: **www.chilel-qigong.com**.

9. Opinion voiced by Martin Rees, Royal Society Research Professor at Cambridge University and quoted in *BBC News* article "Sir Martin Rees: Prophet of Doom?" (April 25, 2003). Website: **http://news.bbc.co.uk/1/hi/in_depth/uk/2000/newsmakers/2976279.stm**.

10. George Musser, "The Climax of Humanity," the introduction to *Crossroads for Planet Earth*, a special edition of *Scientific American* (September 2005). Website: **http://www.sciam.com/issue.cfm?issueDate=Sep-05**.

11. Ibid.

12. Kahlil Gibran, *The Prophet* (New York: Alfred A. Knopf, 1998): p. 56.

13. Coleman Barks, trans., *The Illuminated Rumi* (New York: Broadway Books, 1997): p. 8.

*Chapter 1*

1. Spoken by U.S. Secretary of Defense Donald Rumsfeld during a speech at NATO Headquarters in Brussels, Belgium (June 6, 2002). Website: **http://www. defenselink.mil/transcripts/transcript.aspx?transcriptid=2636.**
2. Lowell A. Goldsmith, "Editorial: Passing the Torch," *Journal of Investigative Dermatology* (2002), on the *Nature* Website: **http://www.nature.com/jid/journal/v118/ n6/full/5601498a.html.**
3. Jay Winsten, Associate Dean and Frank Stanton Director of the Center for Health Communication at the Harvard School of Public Health, "Media & Public Health: Obesity Wars," (May 9, 2005). Website: **http://www.huffingtonpost.com/ jay-winston/media-public-health-ob_b_468.html.**
4. Written by Albert Einstein to his friend Maurice Solovine, February 1951. *The Expanded Quotable Einstein,* Alice Calaprice, ed. (Princeton, NJ: Princeton University Press, 2000): p. 256.
5. Max Planck, from a 1944 speech in Florence, Italy, "Das Wesen der Materie" (The Essence/Nature/Character of Matter). Source: Archiv zur Geschichte der Max-Planck-Gesellschaft, Abt. Va, Rep. 11 Planck, Nr. 1797.
Below I have included a portion of that speech in the original German, with the English translation following.
**Original German:** "Als Physiker, der sein ganzes Leben der nüchternen Wissenschaft, der Erforschung der Materie widmete, bin ich sicher von dem Verdacht frei, für einen Schwarmgeist gehalten zu werden. Und so sage ich nach meinen Erforschungen des Atoms dieses: Es gibt keine Materie an sich. Alle Materie entsteht und besteht nur durch eine Kraft, welche die Atomteilchen in Schwingung bringt und sie zum winzigsten Sonnensystem des Alls zusammenhält. Da es im ganzen Weltall aber weder eine intelligente Kraft noch eine ewige Kraft gibt - es ist der Menschheit nicht gelungen, das heißersehnte Perpetuum mobile zu erfinden - so müssen wir hinter dieser Kraft einen *bewußten intelligenten Geist* annehmen. Dieser Geist ist der Urgrund aller Materie."
**English Translation:** "As a man who has devoted his whole life to the most clear-headed science, to the study of matter, I can tell you as a result of my research about the atoms this much: There is no matter as such! All matter originates and exists only by virtue of a force which brings the particles of an atom to vibration and holds this most minute solar system of the atom together. . . . We must assume behind this force the existence of a conscious and intelligent Mind. This Mind is the matrix of all matter."
6. *The Expanded Quotable Einstein:* p. 220.
7. Mirjana R. Gearhart, "Forum: John A. Wheeler: From the Big Bang to the Big Crunch," *Cosmic Search,* vol. 1, no. 4 (1979). Website: **http://www.bigear.org/ vol1no4/wheeler.htm.**
8. Konrad Zuse, *Calculating Space,* English translation, February 1970. Catalogued as MIT Technical Translation AZT-70-164-GEMIT, Massachusetts Institute of Technology (Project MAC). Website: **http://www.mit.edu.**
9. From the German symposium "Ist das Universum ein Computer?" (Is the Universe a Computer?), November 6–7, 2006. Website: **http://www.dtmb.de/ Webmuseum/Informatikjahr-Zuse/body2_en.html.**
10. Seth Lloyd, *Programming the Universe: A Quantum Computer Scientist Takes On the Cosmos* (New York: Alfred A. Knopf, 2006): p. 3.
11. From an interview with quantum computer scientist Seth Lloyd, "Life, the Universe, and Everything," *Wired,* issue 14.03 (March 2006). Website: **http://www. wired.com/wired/archive/14.03/play.html?pg=4.**
12. Excerpt from *Programming the Universe* describing the universe as a computer on the Random House Website: **http://www.randomhouse.com/catalog/display. pperl?isbn=9781400033867&view=excerpt.**
13. "Life, the Universe, and Everything."
14. Ibid.
15. Ibid.
16. *Programming the Universe:* front-cover flap.

17. John Wheeler during a lecture in 1989, quoted by Kevin Kelly, "God Is the Machine," *Wired,* issue 10.12 (December 2002). Website: **http://www.wired.com/ wired/archive/10.12/holytech.html**.

18. Jürgen Schmidhuber, "A Computer Scientist's View of Life, the Universe, and Everything," *Lecture Notes in Computer Science, vol. 1337: Foundations of Computer Science: Potential—Theory—Cognition,* Christian Freksa, et al., eds. (Berlin: Springer-Verlag, 1997): pp. 201–208. Available on the Dalle Molle Institute for Artificial Intelligence Website: **http://www.idsia.ch/~juergen/everything/node1.html**.

19. Ibid.

20. John Wheeler quoted by John Horgan, *The End of Science: Facing the Limits of Knowledge in the Twilight of the Scientific Age* (London: Abacus, 1998). Website: **http:// suif.stanford.edu/~jeffop/WWW/wheeler.txt**.

21. "The Gospel of Thomas," translated and introduced by members of the Coptic Gnostic Library Project of the Institute for Antiquity and Christianity (Claremont, CA). From *The Nag Hammadi Library,* James M. Robinson, ed. (San Francisco: Harper SanFrancisco, 1990): p. 137.

### Chapter 2

1. John Wheeler, as quoted by F. David Peat in *Synchronicity: The Bridge Between Matter and Mind* (New York: Bantam Books, 1987): p. 4.

2. Ibid.

3. "Quantum Theory Demonstrated: Observation Affects Reality," adapted from a news release by the Weizmann Institute of Science in Rehovot, Israel (February 27, 1998). Website: **http://www.sciencedaily.com/releases/1998/02/980227055013. htm**.

4. H. K. Beecher, "The Powerful Placebo," *Journal of the American Medical Association,* vol. 159, no. 17 (December 24, 1955): pp.1602–1606.

5. Anton J. M. de Craen, Ted J. Kaptchuk, Jan G. D. Tijssen, and J. Kleijnen, "Placebos and Placebo Effects in Medicine: Historical Overview," *Journal of the Royal Society of Medicine,* vol. 92, no. 10 (October 1999): pp. 511–515. Website: **http://www. pubmedcentral.nih.gov/pagerender.fcgi?artid=1297390&pageindex=1**.

6. Margaret Talbot, "The Placebo Prescription," *The New York Times* (January 9, 2000). Website: **http://query.nytimes.com/gst/fullpage.html?res=9C01E6D71E38F 93AA35752C0A9669C8B63&sec=health&spon=&pagewanted=2**.

7. Andy Coghlan, "Placebos Effect Revealed in Calmed Brain Cells," *New Scientist. com* (May 16, 2004). Website: **http://www.newscientist.com/article/dn4996.html**

8. Ibid.

9. Franklin G. Miller, "William James, Faith, and the Placebo Effect," *Perspectives in Biology and Medicine,* vol. 48, no. 2 (Spring 2005): pp. 273–281.

10. "Today's College Students Experience More Anxiety" (June 13, 2007), on the Yale Medical Group Website: **http://www.yalemedical group.org/news/child_607. html**.

11. Ibid.

12. Arthur J. Barsky, et al., "Nonspecific Medication Side Effects and the Nocebo Phenomenon," *Journal of the American Medical Association,* vol. 287, no. 5 (February 6, 2002).

13. Robert and Michèle Root-Bernstein, *Honey, Mud, Maggots, and Other Medical Marvels: The Science Behind Folk Remedies and Old Wives' Tales* (New York: Houghton Mifflin, 1998).

14. Home page for the Framingham Heart Study on the National Heart, Lung, and Blood Institute Website: **http://www.nhlbi.nih.gov/about/framingham/index. html**.

15. Rebecca Voelker, "Nocebos Contribute to Host of Ills," *Journal of the American Medical Association,* vol. 275, no. 5 (February 7, 1996): pp. 345–347.

16. "International Peace Project in the Middle East": p. 778.

17. *Merriam-Webster Online Dictionary.* Website: **http://mw1.merriam-webster. com/dictionary/faith**.

18. Ibid., **http://mw1.merriam-webster.com/dictionary/belief**.

19. Ibid., **http://mw1.merriam-webster.com/dictionary/science**.

20. Albert Einstein quoted by physicist Michio Kaku in an online article, "M-Theory: The Mother of all SuperStrings: An Introduction to M-Theory" (2005). Website: **http://mkaku.org/articles/m_theory.html**.

21. Doc Childre and Howard Martin, with Donna Beech, *The HeartMath Solution: The Institute of HeartMath's Revolutionary Program for Engaging the Power of the Heart's Intelligence* (New York: HarperCollins Publishers, 1999): pp. 33–34.

22. Ibid., p. 24.

23. The shift in energy levels caused by an external magnetic field is called the Zeeman effect. Website: **http://bcs.whfreeman.com/tiplermodernphysics4e/ content/cat_020/zeeman.pdf**.

24. The shift in energy levels caused by an external electric field is called the Stark effect. Website: **http://www.physics.csbsju.edu/QM/H.10.html**.

25. The Institute of HeartMath Research Center conducts basic research on emotional physiology and heart-brain interactions, clinical and organizational studies, and the physiology of learning and optimal performance. These statistics are drawn from an online summary of the communication between the brain and the heart, "Head-Heart Interactions." Website: **http://www.heartmath.org/research/science-of-the-heart/soh_20.html**.

26. Neville, *The Law and the Promise* (Marina del Rey, CA: DeVorss, 1961): p. 44.

27. "The Gospel of Thomas": p. 131.

28. Ibid., p. 137.

29. Rebecca Saxe, "Reading Your Mind: How Our Brains Help Us Understand Other People," *Boston Review* (February/March 2004). Website: **http://bostonreview. net/BR29.1/saxe.html**.

30. *The Law and the Promise:* p. 57.

31. William James, "Does 'Consciousness' Exist?" First published in *Journal of Philosophy, Psychology, and Scientific Methods,* vol. 1 (1904): pp. 477–491. Website: **http://evans-experientialism.freewebspace.com/james_wm03.htm**.

## Chapter 3

1. Daniel C. Dennett, *Consciousness Explained* (Boston: Back Bay Books, 1992): p. 433.

2. The human brain processes information at speeds that range from 100 to 1,000 teraflops (1 teraflop = 1 trillion flops, i.e., 1,000,000,000,000 operations per second). At Indiana University, Big Red (one of the 50 fastest supercomputers in the world) has a theoretical peak performance of more than 20 teraflops, and has achieved more than 15 teraflops on numerical computations.

3. Daniel Goleman, "Pribram: The Magellan of Brain Science," *Psychology Today,* vol. 12, no. 9 (1979): pp. 72f. Website: **http://www.sybervision.com/Golf/ hologram9.htm**.

4. Ibid.

5. Bruce H. Lipton, *The Biology of Belief: Unleashing the Power of Consciousness, Matter, & Miracles* (Santa Rosa, CA: Mountain of Love/Elite Books, 2005): p.166.

6. Spoken by St. Ignatius of Loyola, founder of the Jesuit order, as quoted by Keith Birney, "Give Me a Child . . ." *New Scientist,* issue 2583 (December 23, 2006): p. 2710. Website: **http://www.newscientist.com/article/mg19225832.700-give-me-a-child.html**.

7. William James, *Talks to Teachers on Psychology: and to Students on Some of Life's Ideals* (originally published in 1899; New York: Henry Holt and Company, 1915): p. 77.

8. *The Biology of Belief:* p. 26.

9. Robert Collier (1885–1950) was an American author of a number of books on popular psychology and spirituality, including *The Secret of the Ages, God in You, The Secret of Power, The Magic Word,* and *The Law of the Higher Potential.* A collection of his inspirational quotations can be found at the QuoteLeaf Website: **http://www. inspirationandmotivation.com/robert-collier-quotes.html**.

### Chapter 4

1. "Chill Out: It Does the Heart Good," Duke University news release citing a technical study of the relationship between emotional response and heart health led by Duke University Medical Center researcher James Blumenthal, originally published in *The Journal of Consulting and Clinical Psychology.* Website: **http://Dukemednews. org/news/article.php?id=353**.

2. Brigid McConville, "Learning to Forgive," *Namaste* (July 2000). Hoffman Institute Website: **http://www.quadrinity.com/articles/article4a.htm**.

3."Intense Emotions Can Kill You," *Stress Management Corner,* on the TMI Website: **http://www.tmius.com/6smcorn.HTML**.

### Chapter 5

1. Amanda Dennison's Website: **http://www.firewalks.ca/Press_Release.html**.

2. Alexis Huicochea, "Man Lifts Car Off Pinned Cyclist," *Arizona Daily Star* (July 28, 2006). Website: **http://www.azstarnet.com/sn/printDS/139760**.

3. "Woman Lifts 20 Times Body Weight," *BBC News* (August 4, 2005). Website: **http://news.bbc.co.uk/2/hi/uk_news/england/wear/4746665.stm**.

4. Spoken by Albert Einstein during an address to the Prussian Academy of Sciences in Berlin, Germany, on January 27, 1921. *The Expanded Quotable Einstein:* p. 240.

5. *The Lankāvatāra Sūtra: A Mahayana Text,* D. T. Suzuki, trans., (1932). Website: **http://lirs.ru/do/lanka_eng/lanka-nondiacritical.htm**.

6. *The Divine Matrix:* p. 71.

7. "Quantum Theory Demonstrated: Observation Affects Reality."

8."Forum: John A. Wheeler: From the Big Bang to the Big Crunch."

9. Spoken by Albert Einstein to his student Esther Salaman. *The Expanded Quotable Einstein:* p. 202.

10. Michael Wise; Martin Abegg, Jr.; and Edward Cook, *The Dead Sea Scrolls: A New Translation* (San Francisco: HarperSanFrancisco, 1996): p. 365.

11. Neville, *The Power of Awareness* (Marina del Rey, CA: DeVorss, 1952): p. 98.

12. Ibid.

13. William James (1842–1910) was a pioneering psychologist and the man considered by many to be America's great philosopher. Biography and quotes on Answers Website: **http://www.answers.com/topic/william-james?cat=technology**.

14. *The Power of Awareness:* p. 10.

15. *The Law and the Promise:* p. 9.

16. Ibid., p. 44.

### Chapter 6

1. To learn more about Michael Hedges, visit the Website: **http://www.nomad land.com/Point_A.htm**.

2. William James quoted on ThinkExist Website: **http://www3.thinkexist.com/ quotes/william_james/4.html**.

3. Geoff Heath, "Beliefs and Identity," Bowland Press seminar paper (November 2005). Website: **http://www.bowlandpress.com/seminar_docs/Beliefs_and_ Identity.pdf**.

4. John D. Barrow, "Living in a Simulated Universe," Centre for Mathematical Sciences, Cambridge University. Website: **http://www.simulation-argument.com/ barrowsim.pdf**.

5. *The American Heritage College Dictionary, Third Edition* (Boston: Houghton Mifflin Company, 1977): p. 870.

6. Jonah Lehrer, "Built to Be Fans," *Seed* (Summer 2004): p. 34. Website: **http://www.seedmagazine.com/news/2006/02/built_to_be_fans.php**.

7. Ibid., p. 38.

8. "John 14:12," from the Aramaic of the Peshitta; George M. Lamsa, trans.; *Holy Bible: From the Ancient Eastern Text* (New York: HarperOne, 1985): p.1072.

9. "Built to Be Fans."

10. Jonathan Schaeffer, "Kasparov versus Deep Blue: The Re-match," *International Computer Chess Association Journal,* vol. 20, no. 2 (1997): pp. 95–102. Website: **http://www.cs.vu.nl/~aske/db.html**.


*Chapter 7*

1. Fulke Greville (1554–1628), English poet and philosopher, quoted on Creative Quotations Website: **http://creativequotations.com/one/673.htm**.

2. David Bohm, *Wholeness and the Implicate Order* (London: Routledge, 1980): p. 237.

3. *The American Heritage College Dictionary, Third Edition:* p. 1508.

4. Ibid., p. 1271.

5. Nick Bostrom, "Are You Living in a Computer Simulation?" *Philosophical Quarterly,* vol. 53, no. 211 (2003): pp. 243–255. Website: **http://www.simulation-argument.com**.

6. Ibid.

7. Ibid.

8. Spoken by Stephen Hawking during a speech in Hong Kong, quoted by Sylvia Hui, "Hawking Says Humans Must Colonize Space," *Associated Press* (June 13, 2006). Website: **http://www.space.com/news/060613_ap_hawking_space.html**.

9. "A Computer Scientist's View of Life, the Universe, and Everything."

10. Spoken by Hindu prince Siddhartha Gautama (c. 563 B.C.E.–c. 483 B.C.E.), the Buddha, founder of Buddhism. Website: **http://thinkexist.com/quotation/ all_things_appear_and_disappear_because_of_the/143657.html**.

11. Ibid.

12. *The Prophet:* p. 28.

13. J. Raloff, "Baby's AIDS Virus Infection Vanishes," *Science News,* vol. 147, no. 13 (April 1, 1995): p. 196. Website: **http://www.sciencenews.org/pages/pdfs/ data/1995/147-13/14713-03.pdf**.

# ABOUT THE AUTHOR

*New York Times* best-selling author **Gregg Braden** is internationally renowned as a pioneer in bridging science and spirituality. His ability to find innovative solutions to complex problems led to successful careers as a computer geologist for Phillips Petroleum during the 1970s energy crisis and in the 1980s as a senior computer systems designer for Martin Marietta Aerospace during the last years of the Cold War. In 1991, he became the first technical-operations manager for Cisco Systems, where he led the development of the global support team that assures the reliability of today's Internet.

For more than 20 years, Gregg has searched high mountain villages, remote monasteries, and forgotten texts to uncover their timeless secrets. To date, his work has led to such paradigm-shattering books as *The Isaiah Effect, The God Code, Secrets of the Lost Mode of Prayer,* and *The Divine Matrix.* Now published in 15 languages and 23 countries, Gregg's work shows us beyond any reasonable doubt that we have the power to reverse disease, redefine aging, and even alter reality itself by embracing the power of belief as the quantum language of change.

For further information, please contact Gregg's office at:

Wisdom Traditions
P.O. Box 5182
Santa Fe, New Mexico 87502
(505) 424-6892
Website: **www.greggbraden.com**
E-mail: ssawbraden@aol.com

✳ ✳ ✳